Case Studies in Educational Guidance for Adults

By Linda Butler

with

Judy Midgley
Carole Myers
Freda Tallantyre

GW00545176

National Institute of Adult Continuing Education

Advisory Council for Adult and Continuing Education

19B De Montfort Street Leicester LE1 7GE

CHAIRMAN'S PREFACE

The Advisory Council for Adult and Continuing Education originally made clear its commitment to the development of educational guidance services for adults by publishing in 1979 its report on *Links to learning,* the first full-scale national report to be published on the subject in Britain.

In my preface to that report I wrote: '...the crucial need for accessible information, advice and counselling services has still to be generally acknowledged' and '...such services must be central to future developments in the education of adults'. In the subsequent four years there has been an encouraging shift towards a widening appreciation of the need for guidance services. When *Links to learning* was being drafted there appeared to be about fifteen local guidance services actually in operation. Now there are probably fifty; and that growth has most remarkably been made in a time of recurrent economic crises when the confidence needed to set up new ventures has understandably been at a premium. Perhaps this success against the economic grain of the time is further evidence of the real demand for these services.

Limited as many of these new services are in their funding and organisation their very existence suggests that a further stage has been reached in the consolidation of educational guidance for adults. It was this belief which led the Advisory Council to consider how it might best contribute to this advance. We concluded that it was now time to begin to examine the kind of service enquirers were receiving and their satisfaction with it.

The Council was consequently pleased to discover that the British Library had already instituted a research enquiry into the public library services' provision of educational information and advice which had some similar concerns about 'consumer satisfaction'. It then proved to be only a small step to widen that enquiry, through the addition of research funding from the Advisory Council, so as to take a more detailed look at the complementary sector of educational guidance services for adults. The following report contains the findings of that part of the research project. The larger enquiry into the public libraries' role is covered in a separate report to be published by the British Library.

The Advisory Council is grateful to the British Library for agreeing to our sponsorship of a parallel study within their project. The report, in our view, demonstrates the value of this co-operation which allowed a lot of additional research to be undertaken at a modest cost by an already experienced research team. I emphasise that our funding was relatively small, since this partly explains why our enquiries had to be limited to only four local educational guidance services. Nevertheless those enquiries were very detailed and the services were carefully selected so as to represent a cross-section of the types of services currently operating. Much of the specific findings is therefore gener-alisable to the wider scene.

On behalf of the Council I want to thank the research workers who carried through this study. The enquiry was based in the Open University's regional office in Leeds and directed by Derek Gains, then the deputy director there. Linda Butler formulated the details of the enquiry, supervised the day-to-day work of the three field-workers, Judy Midgley, Carole Myers and Freda Tallantyre, and drafted the final report from their findings. The enquiry was overseen as part of the overall project by an advisory group set up by the British Library and chaired by Sheelagh Watts of the Open University. The Council's representative on that group was Peter Clyne.

The Council is grateful to all those people and especially to the research team for the extremely thorough and competent way in which they carried out the enquiry. Equally we want to thank all the many others, particularly those working in the local services which were studied, who gave so freely of their time and experience to help with the research.

The final outcome of all that effort is the report which follows. The Council, through NIACE, is very pleased to publish it as a first-hand description of the work of educational guidance services and as a valuable appraisal of clients' satisfaction with the services offered. From this data, readers can make their own assessment of the strengths and weaknesses of present provision and how improve-ments might be achieved.

I would only add that the Council is not necessarily to be regarded as subscribing to all or any of the conclusions drawn in it. They are the authors': but we do commend them to the attention of everybody who has an interest in providing educational guidance services for adults.

RICHARD HOGGART
August 1983   Chairman of Council

THE AUTHORS

Linda Butler is a graduate of Nottingham University in politics and psychology, an associate of the Library Association, and a qualified teacher. After teaching in continuing education and research on adult candidates for GCE examinations and on women re-entrants to further education, she was appointed research fellow for the Educational Advisory Services Project at the Open University, Leeds. Her report on this work, *The role of public libraries in the provision of educational guidance for adults* will be published by the British Library in 1984. She is a member of the committee of the National Association of Educational Guidance Services for Adults.

Judy Midgley returned to education as a mature student, first through a Return to Study course and the Open University, then at Bradford University, where she graduated in sociology and social psychology. While an undergraduate, she was asked to become a volunteer with a local EGSA and after training became a counsellor. She conducted a piece of research which examined the different perceptions of the EGSA participants, particularly on the EGSA role as an information service versus a counselling service. She is now a full-time outreach worker in educational guidance.

Carole Myers left school after 'A' levels and held a variety of jobs, resuming part-time study after a number of years. She was eventually admitted as an undergraduate at the University of Hull, where she graduated in psychology. In 1983 she began her PhD studies at the University of Oxford.

Freda Tallantyre is a graduate of the University of London in English language and literature. As a tutor-counsellor for groups of adult students working in the university extra-mural department, the Workers' Educational Association, the Open University and a local Women's Education Programme, she has gained a special awareness of the needs and problems of adults returning to study, particularly the educationally disadvantaged. In 1982 she took up a full-time post as a Workers' Educational Association tutor-organiser.

CONTENTS

PART 3: CONCLUSIONS AND RECOMMENDATIONS

TABLES

Prognosis and outcome

CHAPTER ONE
INTRODUCTION

The Educational Advisory Services Project (EASP), established in October 1980 to analyse the role of public libraries in providing independent* educational guidance for adults, was funded for two years by the British Library and for a further six months, until March 1983, by the Open University. Implicit in the Project's remit was an examination of the relationship between public libraries and independent educational guidance services for adults (EGSAs). The following report is largely based on complementary research undertaken by the Project at the request of, and with funding from, the Advisory Council for Adult and Continuing Education, which asked for a particular enquiry into aspects of the role of EGSAs.

On an immediately pragmatic level, some EGSAs were known to work closely with their local public library service, while others had no more than notional links. An analysis of the modes and mechanics of this cooperation was expected to identify strategies for its development. More fundamentally, there appeared to be considerable similarities in the roles, ethics and clientele of public libraries and EGSAs. As an example, the Project's original research proposal noted that:

> ...Libraries may be seen as a natural source of information for adults, since they are relatively open of access; they are geared to the needs of individual enquirers; they are not competing for potential students and are therefore neutral in terms of offering advice; they are in the business of information storage and retrieval; and already deal with a wide range of enquirers who would not normally find their way to conventional Further Education or Higher Education institutions.

A report from the 1979 conference on 'Partnership: libraries, open learning and adult education' suggested even greater overlap between the work of the two types of agencies:

> ...Recent developments in adult education have revolved around the provision of information and counselling services to assist adults in their choice of educational opportunities. At the same time libraries have been developing community information services which aim to provide local information relevant to their immediate communities in a format acceptable to the people for whom the service is intended. Both professions have engaged in some positive discrimination in favour of people whose educational and/or social background is an inhibiting factor in their take-up of existing services. And both institutions have identified a broader definition of their roles — to encompass a counselling or advisory function.[1]

---

*'Independent' throughout this report means 'independent of any single educational institution or organisation that may be seeking to enrol students for its own courses'. That is a perfectly proper function, of course, but it is not included in this report.

1

By contrast, the ACACE report on *Links to learning* about education-al guidance for adults, also published in 1979, was much more cautious about the role of the public library service. While acknow-ledging their activity in information provision (for example, with the adult literacy campaign) and noting some of the ways they had collaborated in guidance work, the report did not identify public libraries as central contributors to further development:

> ...Librarians have traditionally been approached for information and advice on educational opportunities. In some parts of the country this kind of advice is offered on an informal basis, and a number of librarians would like to see this service extended. The general opinion, however, seems to be that the librarians' responsibility is to arrange referrals to the appropriate information agency.[2]

The Project's first task was therefore to establish the operational and theoretical overlaps (and differences) between public libraries and EGSAs. This was done through visits and interviews with key person-nel in EGSAs and in libraries understood to be particularly attentive to educational guidance. That work, and the literature review also undertaken during this initial period, are the basis of Part 1 of this report. In the interests of brevity, detailed comment on public library provision has not been included, since this is covered in the Project's report on *The role of public libraries in the provision of educational guidance for adults,* published by the British Library.

By the end of this exploratory work, it was apparent that the provision of educational guidance for adults was so relatively new that it had been little researched. In particular, there were no studies of the impact of educational guidance (whether provided by public libraries or EGSAs) on the consumers. The Project proposed to fill this gap through detailed studies of four public libraries' work, from the point of view of the librarians and their enquirers. The ACACE concurrent funding provided for similar studies of four EGSAs, from the viewpoint of the advisers and their clients. This work was done by three fieldworkers; and Part 2 of this report is based on their findings. Again, readers interested in public library research are referred to the Project's report to the British Library.

The Project's exploratory discussions, and the literature review, suggested two distinct types of educational guidance, although in practice they may sometimes overlap. One, concerned with the learner's progress through a course of study, offers support to help cope with difficulties, as for example in the New Opportunities for Women (NOW) courses which contain an in-built guidance element. The other type of educational guidance, usually preceding entry to a course, is concerned to help learners identify and evaluate the most appropriate routes to their chosen educational goal. This is the type of educational guidance mostly offered by EGSAs and public libraries, with EGSAs placing particular emphasis on access to formal provi-

2

sion. The educational guidance provision discussed in this report is principally of this 'directional' kind.

The conclusions and recommendations offered in Part 3 arise from juxtaposing the findings from a preliminary national survey with the detailed practice of four services. Consequently, the Project considers its conclusions and recommendations to have a wider applicability than is suggested by the relatively small number of individual cases which were examined.

Abbreviations and acronyms

ACACE	Advisory Council for Adult and Continuing Education
ALBSU	Adult Literacy and Basic Skills Unit
CAB	Citizens' Advice Bureau
CEP	Community Enterprise Programme
COIC	Careers and Occupational Information Centre
DES	Department of Education and Science
EASP	Educational Advisory Services' Project
EGSA	Educational Guidance Service for Adults
LA	Local Authority
LDCAE	Local Development Council for Adult Education
LEA	Local Education Authority
MSC	Manpower Services Commission
NIAE*	National Institute of Adult Education
NOW	New Opportunities for Women
OU	Open University
PER	Professional and Executive Recruitment
RB	Responsible Bodies
STEP	Short Term Employment Programme
WEA	Workers' Educational Association

---

*Now NIACE   National Institute of Adult Continuing Education (But the new name had not been introduced at the time of this Report).

PART 1: BACKGROUND

CHAPTER TWO

THE DEVELOPMENT OF EDUCATIONAL GUIDANCE SERVICES FOR ADULTS IN THE UK

Introduction

The Project began by reviewing the available literature and talking to key people in independent educational guidance provision. Information was gathered by visits to over thirty EGSAs and more than twenty libraries to get the views of a wide range of practitioners (but not clients), all with substantial experience and expertise in the field. They include public, college and university librarians; full-time EGSA staff; and volunteer EGSA workers drawn from universities (including the Open University), the WEA, polytechnics and colleges, LEA adult education and the careers service. (See Appendix 1 for the interview schedule used).

This exploratory fieldwork was necessary for two reasons. First because, as found by the authors of a review of educational guidance recently published by the National Institute of Adult Education (NIAE):

> ...any form of educational guidance, as a distinct service within adult education, is relatively new, definitions are not universally agreed and research is sparse.[3]

This was particularly true of the directional or route-planning form of educational guidance which was EASP's main area of interest. The aim was therefore to identify and define the components of educational guidance for adults and to examine some models of actual practice, so as to determine the general strengths and weaknesses of each type of service. Thus the Project's initial fieldwork concentrated on the working philosophies and substantive practical issues commonly found by EGSAs, rather than on gathering any detailed information on day-to-day operations. Much of this detailed information had anyway been collected early in 1980 on the twenty services then known to be operational and the two which had recently closed.[4]

The second reason for the exploratory fieldwork was the awareness, through a variety of informal and formal contacts, that there were more EGSAs in operation or planned than were currently listed in the literature. The attitudes and activities of these services had to be examined to make sure that the Project fully covered the range of contemporary practice.

The material collected during this initial phase is presented in Part 1 of the report. This chapter reviews the growth of the EGSAs, examines the ethos of the movement, comments on some models for EGSA provision, and considers three critical operational matters. The practice of educational guidance, in terms of definitions, justifications, operational goals and the extent to which they are achievable, is examined in Chapter 3.

Numbers of EGSAs

Belfast

Probably the first independent EGSA in the UK was established in Belfast in 1970. The Belfast EGSA had opened three years before as the Adult Vocational Guidance Service. Although the Service had from the beginning offered educational as well as vocational guidance,

> ...it was soon apparent that a greater need was in broader educational information and guidance. When the vocational aspect was partially met by the setting up....of Occupational Guidance Units, it was possible to shift the Service's orientation firmly towards adult education...[5]

Others, on the mainland, were slow to follow. In 1979, ACACE's *Links to learning* report listed only fifteen EGSAs, with a further three at an advanced planning stage. That picture presents a slight distortion of the Services started, since a few had been forced to close, sometimes through failure to attract long-term funding: an important example was the ERIC venture in Cardiff. Such closures attracted considerable attention among those working in educational guidance for adults, and in the early 1980s there was much anxiety that some of these would disappear:

> ...we are at a critical period for information and guidance services. The Merseyside Educational Guidance Service for Adults has had to close down; others are under threat; some are hanging on by the skin of their teeth.[6]

However, the Project's research actually revealed a surprising growth in numbers between 1979 and 1982. Its first *Directory*, published in 1981 in conjunction with ACACE, listed thirty-three EGSAs in operation or at an advanced planning stage;[7] its second, in 1982, listed forty-five;[8] the third, in 1983, listed forty-nine.[9] This increase in numbers was accompanied by a degree of stability. Though individual EGSAs might indeed feel precarious, there were few closures between 1980 and 1982; and while most of the Services were entirely new ventures, a few were unearthed during our research which had been in existence for some years.

The list of EGSAs in the Project's 1983 Directory shows that while some areas of the country, such as London, are now reasonably well served, others have no provision.[9] There have been many calls for a more comprehensive and systemised provision. Michaels, for example, envisaged a statutory service 'modelled on the reorganised Careers Advisory Service'[10] and most recently ACACE has sought

> ...to encourage all local education authorities and other providing agencies to cooperate in the early establishment and continued support of local educational guidance services for adults.[11]

There has been no national initiative in response to these calls, although the National Association of Educational Guidance Services, formed in 1982, has made a major priority of encouraging the development of Services in areas with little or no provision.

EGSAs cannot claim to be the only bodies in the UK offering educational guidance to adults. Both *Links to learning* and the NIAE's review stress the great variety of organisations able to offer at least information (and often more) to adults. The NIAE review comments that:

> ...there was a tendency, because of the natural interest in particular and existing schemes, to lose a sense of the relative scale of providing institutions or bodies operations. As far as we can estimate from the evidence, in 1977/78, the Local Authority Careers Service was the major provider dealing with some 100,000 clients although only a small proportion of these would have been adults seeking educational advice specifically; the Manpower Services Commission was the second major provider, dealing with some 60,000 (at least). The evidence suggests that these two bodies also dealt with the largest number of clients so far as counselling is concerned; as an estimate, some 40,000 by the Local Authority Careers Service, some 4,000 to 5,000 by the Manpower Services Commission.[12]

On the other hand, it is apparent that the central commitment of Careers Services and of the Manpower Services Commission (MSC) is to careers and vocational guidance, while EGSAs' is to educational guidance. There are many educational guidance agencies which offer help to specific target groups defined by level/clientele (for example, the Higher Education Advisory Service); but EGSAs normally adopt a broadly-based, generalist stance. Most educational providers offer information and advice about their own courses, but again they are not generalist agencies; and the neutrality of these sources may be open to question. EASP's exploratory fieldwork suggested that EGSAs offered a unique focus, range and approach. Thus, a number of criteria were applied to services to be included in the *Directories*. These were that the EGSA offered guidance independently of the interests of supporting institutions and that educational guidance was its primary function; that it offered most, if not all, the guidance functions of information, assessment, advice, counselling and implementation; that it was aimed primarily at the general public, not at existing in-house students or very specific groups, such as ex-offenders; and that guidance should be available across the whole range of continuing education. Implicit in these criteria was an emergent ethos of educational guidance for adults.

Ethos of the EGSA movement

The emergence of an EGSA ethos has been closely bound up with the main developments in continuing education throughout the 1970s. A number of major reports identified independent educational guidance for adults as a key factor in enhancing access to continuing education.

In 1973, the Russell Report pointed to:

> ...the advantages of established adult education centres as points of enquiry about any matter relating to the education of adults or the cultural resources of the area. Help of this kind, to enable the individual to identify and locate the most suitable activity for his educational needs, is an essential component of a comprehensive service of adult education and one which the full-time staff of adult education institutions will be constantly called on to furnish. Such action is sometimes referred to as counselling. We believe that term is better reserved for the full guidance services that are being developed in certain other sectors of education. These, which use trained counsellors and accepted diagnostic approaches, are distinct from the information services that we are here considering. To establish a true counselling service for adult education would be a costly and elaborate undertaking with heavy training demands, for inexpert counselling is potentially harmful. We cannot recommend the diversion of resources in that direction at the present time, but we do emphasize the importance of an adequate information service at every adult education centre, especially at those times of year when new activities are beginning. It should contain three elements: access to the fullest possible information about education and cultural activities open to adults both locally and through residential study; ready contact with existing counselling services, including vocational guidance, for those who appear to need it; and an opportunity for the individual enquirer to clarify his choice for himself through discussion with someone informed about all the possibilities. This, whilst a long way short of counselling (and it is vital that the difference be recognised) is not a task for a clerical assistant but for the professional adult education staff and it should figure appropriately in their training.[13]

While this statement accurately reflects the facilities that many EGSAs claimed in their evidence to EASP to offer their clients, it does not reflect the concern of some that a Service within educational institutions might present two major problems: (a) that such institutions might be perceived as threatening and impersonal and be little used by adults unused to their ways; and (b) that educational institutions were not necessarily the best places to seek objective advice, since many would have their own interests at heart, not those of the enquirer.

The broadening of access to education for sections of the population previously debarred — because of lack of formal qualifications or of appropriate kinds of provision — was at the heart of the creation of the Open University. In noting:

> ...a paradigm shift in the thinking of adult educators about the role in access to educational opportunities of information, advice and counselling

Percy et al. comment that, 'The Open University must be credited as a prime mover'.[14] Its commitment to broad-ranging and impartial information advice and counselling, both pre- and post-entry (as well as to on-going guidance for its students), has been reflected in its continuing support of many EGSAs. Of particular note was the University's concern, voiced in the 1976 Venables Report, that such Services should be based on cooperation between all relevant providers, 'with a view to the broadening of access and advice'. Two essential elements identified were:

(a) a commitment on the part of providers in the locality to collaborate in the service (and these include LEAs, RB, local representatives of national bodies, LA Careers Service, OU, PER, and so on)

(b) volunteer support from contributing agencies to extend the reach of the service (in sheer hours, manning the advice team, and in moving out towards major points of contact in the adult community)

and it also noted:

...there is a trend away from dependence on particular educational institutions, sometimes towards using town centre advice offices (Citizens Advice Bureaux, local Councils of Social Service and Public Libraries).[15]

The Open University's concern was replicated in other areas of ~~ABE~~ continuing education. For example, experience with adult literacy provision showed many of its students to have similar needs and led the Adult Literacy and Basic Skills Unit (ALBSU) to fund experimental guidance services geared to adult basic education, in the late 1970s. *what*

Such developments reflected a growing conviction that, even with *stops* more flexible entrance requirements and more 'relevant' course *adults* content, adults considering returning to education were deterred by the difficulty of finding and understanding the information they needed; by limited assessment of their abilities (perhaps based on success or failure at school); by the difficulty of finding reliable advice on their best course of action; by the complexity of matching educational aspirations with domestic responsibilities and vocational needs; and by the bureaucratic nature of educational institutions and their admissions procedures in particular. Such considerations again pointed to a collaborative model for the provision of educational guidance. By this means, the adult enquirer might be placed at the centre of the negotiation, able to select from the full range of institutions' offerings and aided by advisers free of institutional bias. Educational guidance was seen as essentially client-centred, not institution-centred.

It was on this basis that many independent educational guidance services came into existence. Arguments justifying expenditure on educational guidance were an interesting mix of altruism and expediency. *Links to learning,* the first national report on provision, reflected very clearly these two elements in the debate:

...Guidance services in continuing education should provide a two-way process, in which educators can promote their existing provision and learn about new demands. Selling what continuing education has to offer is an important reason for establishing guidance services, but it should not be the operating principle.[16]

11

That EGSAs might have a role in enabling continuing educators to 'learn about new demands' takes the principle of client-centredness one step further and towards that of advocacy. Both found clear expression in the development through the 1970s of educational brokerages in the United States:

> One distinctive quality of brokering agencies is that they aim to present adults with the complete range of educational and career alternatives and help them choose those most appropriate to their individual needs. Brokering agencies are neutral towards the choices made; conventional educational institutions usually aim to increase their own clientele or student bodies... What is distinct about brokering is the packaging and delivery systems for these services — the ways clients are reached and served directly in the community — and, perhaps most important, the new educational role of client advocate. Client advocacy means placing learners' needs and interests above those of the institutions. This advocacy for clients' interests takes two forms: intercession on behalf of individual students, and efforts to change individual policies which hamper adult learners' re-entry and progress: e.g. scheduling, offerings, costs...[17]

These arguments for the autonomous agency with a political role have found champions in Britain. Many of the EGSAs set up in the early 1980s were shop-front or other 'neutral' premises (as opposed to institution-based premises). It is argued that they demonstrate to the educational institutions themselves that the guidance offered is bias-free and not a covert recruitment agency for any one host institution; and that they reinforce the guidance workers' feelings of independence and facilitate the client advocacy role. In these respects, some services represent another facet of the client-centred and community-based advice and advocacy movement which became established in the United Kingdom in the 1970s.

Thus, as it has developed through the 1970s and into the 1980s, educational guidance for adults has become increasingly associated with the linked values of improved access, collaborative provision, independence, client-centredness and advocacy.

Models of EGSA provision

The Project found that EGSAs' structures were closely in line with the three models identified in *Links to learning*, whose descriptions are therefore quoted here in full:

> ...The Link Chain. This type relies on volunteer staff drawn either from adult educators and counsellors or more generally from professionals in other fields; some services include volunteers recruited from the general public. The service is made known through directories naming the volunteers within the link chain. Potential students can be referred to the most appropriate person in the chain. This model is seemingly cheap to establish, as costs are often absorbed by the institutions providing the volunteers. It also makes it possible to serve areas with a large and

scattered population which could not readily be served by a centralised service. There is, however, no organising centre feeding accurate and up-to-date information to the links making up the chain and no simple point of contact for the public. Volunteers are often unwilling to keep comprehensive records. While this type of service is potentially helpful to those who gain access to it, and has ready-made mechanisms for feedback to the educational system, it can be somewhat haphazard in practice.[18]

This description of the strengths and weaknesses of the model appear to us to hold good, except that the link-chain may well have an organising centre for information, however small-scale, and that volunteers are most likely to be professional continuing educators.

2
...The Centre. This type is a centralised service, often with trained personnel, providing services on a professional basis. There is a single point of contact with the public, which makes access theoretically easy, although the service has to be in a city centre if it is to be conveniently located for large numbers of people. The closeness of its links with other institutions is determined by the service's philosophy. This type is probably very effective from the client's point of view, although it may not incorporate any means of encouraging change in education provision.[19]

Centre-type EGSAs located in educational institutions are likely to be full-time or part-time staffed by professional continuing educators. Those in other locations are likely to be full-time staffed by persons from a variety of the 'caring' professions (including, of course, education). Both may also use temporary MSC-funded personnel. We heard arguments which suggested that EGSAs located in educational institutions might well be effective in 'encouraging change', particularly in their own institution, and dependent on their status and reputation within it. The standing of centre-type EGSAs in other locations affected the degree to which they could also achieve change (some were highly successful), while they were most likely to be active in advocacy.

3
...The Link-Chain-Centre. This type aims to combine the positive features of the other two. The link chain uses existing resources of personnel, information, and other services; the organising centre may provide counsellor training, a standard format for assessment, and a single point of contact for the public. The centre uses the link chain for referrals. Volunteers in the chain can become outreach workers, establishing the service at a local level. This model can succeed only through cooperation between existing education and guidance agencies to generate extra resources where these cannot be provided by the individual agencies. The client-centred nature of its approach depends on the organising centre's effect on volunteer staff through training and through co-operative methods.[20]

We found that link-chain-centre-type Services were most commonly sited in 'neutral' premises and that increasingly they were staffed by temporary MSC-funded appointees. They usually arose from link-chain Services concerned to offer a more continuous and visible presence to the public and to offer stronger information and administrative support to links. We heard arguments to suggest that the establishment of a central organisation might decrease links' commitment to the EGSA. In such circumstances, training assumed an important role in maintaining links' motivation, and was in any case necessary to ensure that MSC staff could work effectively.

4   A fourth model may be distinguished which differs from the three outlined, not in structure but in mode of operation. This is the distance-guidance model, probably a centre or link-chain-centre, but which operates primarily *via* telephone, post or radio.

These four models indicate the range of ways in which EGSAs are structured and operated, but it seems clear that generally they are moving towards a centre structure, supported by a strong referral network. This point is confirmed in the findings of a small-scale questionnaire survey conducted by Patterson in 1982 and based on response from twenty-three Services:

> ...The three broad models of operation outlined in *Links to learning* ('link-chain', 'the centre' and 'link-chain-centre') seem less appropriate now with sixteen of the twenty-three services examined falling, by and large, into the centre type service and the remainder under the umbrella of the link-chain-centre model.[21]

Some operational issues

Among a number of operational issues recurring in discussions held with key EGSA personnel, three stood out as particularly problematic. They were finance, staffing and location; and they are briefly reviewed here. Each also has a detailed bearing on the practice described in Chapter 4.

1
Finance   Securing adequate funding is a matter which has bedevilled EGSAs since their inception, affecting even the longest-established and internationally-known Service, the Belfast EGSA, whose threatened closure precipitated a Northern Ireland Department of Education Report in 1979. The Report's comments on securing funding apply to many Services still:

> ...many of the guidance services recently established elsewhere in the United Kingdom are still in the experimental stage and have no guaranteed long-term financial support. Indeed some have been largely dependent for their staffing on the one-year Job Creation Projects sponsored by the Manpower Services Commission, on 'one-off' grants from various bodies or on temporary secondment arrangements sometimes associated with redundancies elsewhere. Local authorities seem on the whole more able to help with loan of premises and assistance with support services and publicity than with the salaries of counselling staff.[22]

The situation has improved, with mainstream funding now available for some Services, particularly those in the London area, and the Belfast EGSA itself now enjoys 90% grant aid from the Department of

Education for Northern Ireland. Indeed, the growth in numbers of EGSAs leads us to believe that to say 'All have their inbuilt insecurities producing a prolonged drift downwards or abrupt closure'[23] is overstating the case. Nevertheless, the view that a Service 'will not be able to fill its potential — not because the validity of the work is questionable but because there is not enough money in the kitty'[24] seems genuinely applicable to many EGSAs. Link-chain Services may find their 'hidden' resources less and less easy to hide. Centres in 'neutral' premises may spend much time in negotiating for grant and maintenance of funds, while those in educational premises may find their resources cut back or be faced with redevelopment. Link-chain-centres depend greatly on MSC policy and so face continuing insecurity.

Staffing is of course related to funding, since funding determines the number and type of staff bought in. It seems to us that the link-chain-centre and link-chain models provide a strategy that attempts to minimise the lack of sufficient full-time trained staff to man a central point and offer outreach. This strategy places much responsibility on volunteers — who do not always have sufficient expertise or access to training. (Indeed, the same applies to many full-time staff, particularly MSC-funded appointees). This has led some EGSAs to limit their range of functions. The difficulty may be that clients do not necessarily limit their needs.

Location is a question that has raised ethical issues, since there is strong feeling in some EGSAs that providing independent guidance from particular educational institutions is not practicable. In our view, the critical issues are the attitudes of the EGSA personnel and their relationship to the host institution, rather than the location itself, and pressure from sponsors is not limited to EGSAs in this type of location. A more relevant issue is the physical and psychological accessibility of the Service's premises. It will be recalled that a major argument against locating a Service in educational premises is that the institution itself may appear threatening to those not used to it. Similar arguments have been applied to public libraries. But advocates of shop front or other 'neutral' premises face the difficulty that prime-site, ground-floor accommodation is expensive. They may well find themselves having to use locations that are not only uninviting to look at but also difficult to find. For them, funding is again at the heart of the matter.

Funding is not the sole factor inhibiting EGSAs' development. Educational guidance for adults is relatively new and its functions are still subject to dispute among its practitioners. But inadequate and highly insecure funding were cited time and again as causing insurmountable problems which led to compromises of practice. It has been aptly said that:

...support Services for adult learners, however, are never as popular with administrators, government officials, and other funders nor as visible to the general public, as are the educational programmes themselves.[25]

Nearly ten years after the Russell Report, ACACE still found it necessary to call for 'small sums of extra public expenditure to provide educational guidance services for adults...'[26]

While there has been some movement, especially in London, towards Services being 'financed in ways which make coherent planning possible',[27] our evidence firmly indicates the continued marginality of most Services, a fact which has certainly had its impact on practice.

CHAPTER THREE
PRACTICE: SOME TERMS, DEFINITIONS AND ISSUES

Introduction

The purpose of this chapter is to define the main components of educational guidance and to outline the justifications made for each component; to examine the operational goals implied; and to review the extent to which Services are able to meet these goals. It is based on the exploratory fieldwork conducted by the Project (described in Chapter 2) and edited from its Interim Report,[28] to which readers seeking greater detail are referred. It should be noted that our evidence at this stage was collected from those providing educational guidance and not from its consumers. The chapter thus offers a composite of practitioners' views on the ideals and actualities of educational guidance.

The main areas of clients' needs identified are:
(i) adequate *information* and help in interpreting that information;
(ii) a full array of appropriate options and assistance where necessary in making a choice (*advice*);
(iii) help in elucidating her or his own needs, capabilities, aspirations and potentialities (*assessment and counselling*);
(iv) assistance in *implementing* her or his goal.

Particular attention has been paid to defining each of these functions since our fieldwork underlined the pertinence of a point made in *Links to learning*:

> ...at present too many agencies attempt to provide some or all of these functions in a haphazard and unconsidered way. This is not to say that these functions can easily be separated in practice, nor that they should be provided by different agencies, but it is important that they should be distinguished clearly in the minds of the providers.[29]

In line with *Links to learning*'s usage, the term 'guidance' has been chosen to encompass all these activities, but we have preferred 'implementation' to 'enabling', since all the activities under consideration may be considered enabling.

Information

Information is here defined as Service-input material about educational provision and availability, which may comprise 'hard' data (the time and venue of a particular class, for example) and/or 'soft' data (for instance, the degree of formality or informality characteristic of an institution's approach to the adult learner). Many EGSAs attempt to bring together all the required information about learning opportunities in the area. Such a facility is of particular importance to the adult. While it may be hard enough for a school-pupil to make the right educational choice, s/he may well have access to expert assistance and peer support, neither of which is likely to apply to the adult re-entrant. Additionally, post-school education is very complex; there are more subjects, more types and levels of qualifications, more modes of attendance, complicated fees and grants structures to consider. These factors apply whether the intention is to develop a leisure interest or to pursue a career objective. Moreover, adults carry with them the accumulated benefits and burdens of their personal histories: commitments to people, to a job, to a particular area. These may rule out the better-known forms of provision, such as the evening class or the full-time degree course. Besides, what adults 'know' of educational provision for the mature person may be based on what they learned, or did not learn, at school thirty years before; innovations in adult education (more open access to higher education and educational credit transfer are examples) are seldom well-publicised. Therefore, we suggest that complete information implies information which is comprehensive, accurate, objective and readily accessible.

Comprehensive information implies first of all that coverage of all local educational opportunities open to adults, whether vocational or general (non-vocational), is offered. While evidence suggests that most adults want local provision, the definition of locality depends on each individual's circumstances; a mother of young children will probably not regard a day-centre fifteen miles away as local. It also depends on the geography and transport network of the area, rather than on single institutional catchment areas or LEA boundaries. In addition, a regional and national perspective needs to be maintained, since a minority of enquirers (typically in their twenties and single) are likely to want information on higher education or training, which may be outside the locality. Secondly, comprehensive information implies coverage that is prospective as well as current; knowing whether a course will be offered in the following academic year is essential in planning an educational programme. Thirdly, comprehensiveness suggests offering a range of information covering many originating providers, since many educational opportunities are offered by organisations other than the statutory providers (private institutions, employers and trade unions, clubs and societies are examples). Fourthly, it implies that the range of information also covers modes of study; for example, a correspondence course may be more appropriate than a part-time course requiring regular weekly attendance. Fifthly, comprehensive information implies not only range but depth. Adult learners may need sufficient detail to identify the provision most appropriate to their personal circumstances: about location, start-time, duration, costs, fees and grants, creches and other enabling facilities, and enrolment procedures. They may need information to identify the level of course most appropriate to their current competence: about course content, its level, the skills (including formal qualifications) that are demanded on entry, explanations about qualifications and their subsequent use. They may need sufficient information to identify the most suitable mode of teaching and learning: and about assessment methods.

Our second criterion is accuracy. It is at the least discouraging and irritating to be given information which is inaccurate or misleading; but the consequences of misinformation may be irretrievably bad. Our third criterion is objectivity. A UNESCO Symposium Report points to the problem: 'Legitimate publicity, including recruiting, should be distinguished from unscrupulous and misleading marketing'.[30] But the dividing line is difficult to draw; many brochures and prospectuses are primarily marketing tools. Such material might in any case be supplemented by information about the quality of the course under consideration; the student support offered; and the recruitment needs and policies of specific institutions.

Accessible information of course implies physical accessibility. It also implies that the arrangement and presentation of the information accords with the user's needs. Most adults are unlikely to have any broad understanding of the structure of continuing education, so arrangement by institution or on hierarchical principles is not generally helpful. Accessibility also implies information which is attractive to read.

So the information requirements in educational guidance are certainly daunting; but the quality of this information base determines to a large extent the scope of the other guidance functions, most emphatically assessment and advice. In any case, many EGSAs reported that information enquiries formed the bulk of their work-load.

Establishing and maintaining such an information base is beset by problems. In the first place there appear to be three levels of educational information. Public level information is what is made available for public consumption by providing institutions and organisations. Obvious examples are brochures and prospectuses. Semi-public level information is what providers will normally offer if asked, most readily (though not exclusively) to co-professionals. A college's decision on the future provision of a particular course is an example. Private level information is what is not formally offered, either to co-professionals or to members of the public: for example, opinions on the quality of a particular course or the competence of an individual teacher. It is perhaps a characteristic peculiar to educational information that so much of what may be relevant to fully informing an enquirer is held to be outside the public level domain. It is, of course, obvious that no EGSA operates without at least basic public level information; and some have developed a most comprehensive range of source material and great competence in obtaining, storing, retrieving and interpreting it. Many feel, however, that the pursuit of semi-public level and private level information is rarely feasible and possibly unwise. Private level information in particular is seen as problematic. It is generally dependent on subjective judgments and potentially disruptive of carefully nurtured personal contacts. On the other hand, those EGSAs which have developed their private level information give it a high value. An EGSA's policy in providing public and private level information depends on guiding principles, local conditions, relationships and available resources.

Secondly, there is dispute over the range of information which should be carried. For example, many Services give little or no attention to commercial providers: with implications for alternative modes of study, since these often come within the private sector. While it may be argued that a full range of information is an essential feature of the enquirer-centred service, as opposed to the institution-centred service, often the problem is a pragmatic one. Some Services are under pressure to demonstrate value for money, i.e. numbers of enquirers referred to each supporting institution. Under these circumstances, with the highly limited funding characteristic of such Services, it is perhaps not surprising that their efforts are concentrated on public sector provision. But the stance may also be a matter of principle, to support the public sector wherever possible. Some Services excluding commercial sector information do so on the grounds that it is usually much more expensive than clients can afford and that the quality of this provision may well be open to doubt. However, we consider that these judgments are finally more rightly ones to be made by the client rather than by the EGSA on the client's behalf.

Thirdly, the question of who should be responsible for the provision of adequate information is another problem. At the public information level, Services place heavy reliance on individual institutions' brochures and prospectuses, while their experience with these sources show them often to be imperfect. They are sometimes hard to obtain; they often arrive too late for peak demand; some of the information will already be out-of-date and more will become so as the year progresses; and they frequently lack the kind of detail that EGSAs know their public demands. They may also be couched in difficult language; be unwieldy in format; lack internal logic or even an index. Hence, some EGSAs find that one of their major tasks is supplementing and interpreting public-level information by direct negotiation with individual institutions. Other Services maintain that only those in charge of a course are able to provide full and accurate public-level information, which such contacts may well supplement with semi-public and private information. Those with this view rely heavily on referral. Some Services do not see information provision as an important function, viewing it as essentially a low-grade clerical task. Where staff time is scarce, it is better devoted to the 'professional' tasks of advice and counselling. Enquirers, it is felt, can reasonably be expected to find information for themselves; but they cannot advise or counsel themselves.

Cumulatively, these three fundamental issues call into question whether it is fully possible, even given adequate funding, to offer educational information which is comprehensive, accurate, objective and accessible. This remains so even with such desirable developments as computerised data-bases and greater institutional co-operation: during 1980-82, we heard of a number of experiments using computerised systems to store educational information.

Assessment

'Assessment' has been usefully defined by Watts as 'making a diagnostic judgment about the client's suitability for certain options'.[31] Many adults' last exposure to formal public assessment of their suitability for certain educational options took place at eleven years. Moreover, given the discrediting of the eleven plus as a fully reliable method of selection; the predominance of early specialisation in the school system; the personal developments and declines specific to adulthood; differential access to educational training and career opportunities dependent on sex, social class, occupation and other factors; the enormous changes both in the range and content of educational training and careers opportunities open to adults; changing patterns of employment and under- or unemployment; and the difficulties inherent in self-assessment; then the adult learner's need for assessment and re-assessment appear great.

The facilities and conditions needed to provide adequate assessment are first, access to an appropriately-trained assessor (and, where necessary, to psychometric tests and other tools) to elucidate the individual's relevant personal history, present circumstances, abilities, potentialities and aspirations; second, that such assessment should be offered in an independent context, that is, uncoloured by the personal biases of the assessor or by the recruitment targets of individual institutions; and third, that the assessor should be adequately informed about the range and nature of educational opportunities on offer. It may be that an assessor is presented with a number of possible options for, or more likely by, a particular client, and asked to make a diagnostic judgment on the client's suitability for each. In that case, an understanding of what each of those options entails is crucial. Alternatively, an assessor may be presented with the task of building up an array of appropriate options on the basis of the diagnosis s/he makes of the client. Again, a grasp of existing provision is crucial in the process. These points are particularly important where adviser and assessor are the same person, and where, as a consequence, discrepancies of judgment are unlikely to be revealed in the process of case discussion.

The availability of educational assessment facilities to the general public, where the starting point is the client's needs, not the institution's, is currently very limited. There appears to be a critical gap in provision; how far are EGSAs able to fill that gap? Two key issues here both relate to diagnosis. The first concerns the ways in which diagnosis is made. Very few Services offer psychometric testing to their enquirers, and then only to a minority of them. (A few more make occasional use of such tools as self-completion forms to test occupational interest, a technique borrowed from the Careers Service). Many Services object to psychometric testing in principle, arguing that the tests themselves are unreliable and that clients may well be fearful of them and hence deterred from coming to the Service. Those employing such tools take a different view. At the Belfast Service, for example,

> ...while testing is seen, not as 'magic', but as a useful tool giving clients objective information about their abilities, the Service feels that it is of prime importance, particularly in assessing the potential of adults with little formal educational background or prior attainments, in examining special abilities and disabilities, and in promoting confidence in the accuracy of the assessments offered. The staff would be unwilling to function without this system.[32]

In most Services, however, diagnosis depends largely on less measurable methodologies, which may include enquirer self-assessment and the exercise of the guidance worker's intuition, knowledge and experience.

The second issue concerns what data about the enquirer are taken into account in the process of diagnosis. Her/his educational and vocational history and aspirations; competences, aptitudes and personality; and personal (including financial and family) circumstances may or may not be given consideration. It is, of course, not unreasonable to exclude certain methodologies or data from the process of diagnosis. The enquirer may not wish it: several EGSAs voiced scruples about intruding into the enquirer's personal domain. There are, moreover, a number of Services which do not claim to offer objective assessment, but rather view themselves as responding to enquirer self-assessment. On the other hand, it is very difficult to exclude some diagnostic judgment about the enquirer's suitability for certain options from the process of educational guidance; and obvious dangers arise where an EGSA's workers are not fully aware of making such judgments or are making them from an inadequate understanding of the client's background. These dangers are magnified by the typically limited exposure which staff currently have to training in the dynamics and skills of assessment.

Advice and counselling
In the context of continuing education, advice, counselling and even guidance itself are disputed terms. The choice of 'guidance' as the Project's generic term is not universally agreed; for example, some

Services have avoided it since it may connote in the public's mind that users have 'a problem' (cf marriage guidance) and a similar consideration applies to the use of counselling. Some Services appear to use the term 'guidance' to indicate that counselling is not offered; another makes a distinction in its title between guidance, which is held to be directive, and counselling, which is held to be non-directive. The use of 'advice' is avoided by some Services on the grounds that it suggests, misleadingly, that evaluations of the quality of courses will be made (cf Consumer Advice Centres). Some use the term to indicate that the emphasis in their provision is on helping people to understand the variety of options open to them, rather than on providing detailed information or counselling; others eschew the word entirely, feeling that it connotes imposition, partiality and directiveness. This widely-varying use of terms is reflected in much of the literature on educational guidance; readers should beware of assuming that there is consensus.

In particular, advice and counselling are often used interchangeably; but we consider that there are substantive differences between them. Advice may be defined as the process of facilitating the learner's choice-making through a mediator who selects and/or reviews the learner's options and who may suggest or recommend an appropriate path or paths.

The following typology of advice-giving is suggested. First, the arraying of the full range of relevant educational options and an analysis of the advantages and disadvantages of each may be termed complete and non-directive advice. Second, recommendations on the most appropriate option to choose from that full range may be termed complete and directive advice. Third, the arraying of a narrow band from the full array of relevant options and an analysis of the advantages and disadvantages of each one may be termed incomplete and non-directive advice. Fourth, recommending as most appropriate an option from that narrow band may be termed incomplete and directive advice.

So defined, advice-giving differs from educational counselling in a number of ways. Effective advice depends on having a client who is already at the point where s/he is able to be receptive to it; educational counselling is appropriately offered to the client who is not yet at that point. In advice, the range of options from which selection may be made can be fairly readily determined; counselling is concerned with helping the client to identify the nature and extent of that range. The role of the adviser is to act as an expert resource mediator, the client as a recipient, active or passive; the role of the counsellor is to act jointly with the client, to facilitate identification and articulation of his or her needs. These three criteria demonstrate that educational counselling (but not advising) is characteristically developmental and permits of the monitoring of change in the individual concerned.

23

Thus, in theoretical terms at least, the distinction between advice and counselling is not that the former is directive and the latter non-directive. Advice-giving may well be non-directive, and, in any case, we heard evidence to suggest that the counselling used in educational guidance is most likely to be directive in nature. Educational counselling is strongly information-based and the counsellor may well take a directive part in the process — for instance, by pointing the client to an appropriate course of action and enabling the client to pursue that course.

Three main reasons why adults seek advice were delineated: (i) the available routes and goals may be unknown or where they are known very complex; (ii) the learner may lack self-assurance and so seek an expert opinion on the appropriateness of certain aspirations; and (iii) the learner may believe that semi-public or private-level information, to which s/he feels the chosen expert will have access, may have an important bearing on decision-making.

We found that it was difficult to determine the extent to which Services engaged in advice-giving, because of the problems of definition discussed earlier. Certainly many EGSA personnel preferred to describe a discursive element in client contact, rather than a directive one. Yet in our view, directiveness may often be appropriate in practice. Recommending a particular option (i.e. directive advice-giving) may be a perfectly reasonable response to directive advice-seeking; and it may be an imposition to refuse to give directive advice in certain circumstances. Moreover, it is not difficult to envisage situations where unsolicited directive advice is absolutely proper. An example might be telling someone making enquiries about studying 'O' levels by correspondence to check whether s/he will be able to sit the examination locally. Nor is complete advice (the arraying of the full range of possible options) necessarily superior practice to incomplete advice (the arraying of a narrow band of options from the full range). The enquirer may specifically ask for or prefer to deal only with a narrow range of options.

We argue, then, that advice is an integral part of educational guidance and that no one form of advice, directive or non-directive, complete or incomplete, is intrinsically superior to another. Certain conditions must apply here, however. The first is an adequate and easily-accessed information bank from which to draw out relevant options. Incomplete advice should be seen as an informed and positive judgment; incomplete advice which arises from inadequacies in the information base or the adviser's own lack of knowledge *should be declared to be so.* Secondly, competent advice-giving requires staff who are trained to recognise the processes of enquirer assessment in which they may be engaged. Thirdly, directive advice should be an informed and positive judgment, and not just a vehicle for institutional partiality or personal bias. Directive advice which is coloured to any extent by the adviser's biases should be *declared to be so* to the enquirer. Fourthly, staff need to be competent to recognise the difference between information, advice and counselling need, so far as this is possible.

Centre-type, full-time staffed EGSAs appeared most likely to give detailed and in-depth advice. For the others, early referral was normal practice. In fact, all Services claimed well-developed strategies to deal with much advice through the establishment of networks of contacts into individual educational establishments. The need for this form of outreach is very apparent. Few Services enjoy sufficient staff continuity, time or expertise to offer immediate and detailed advice on the vast range of continuing education provision. In many cases, the worker's sole source of information about a particular option was providing institutions' brochures or prospectuses. Hence some of the antipathy to the notion of advice-giving, since for many EGSA personnel it connoted a depth of evaluation which they were not in a position to provide.

Conceptually, educational guidance is a cluster, not a linear process, and in terms of good practice counselling cannot be omitted. However, only a small number of Services appear to offer counselling in the sense outlined above. Often the term appears to be used to describe a process of thoughtful advice-giving, informed by some counselling techniques. It was difficult, in fact, to determine the extent to which adult learners need counselling. Nearly all Services report that such enquirers are in a minority. The extent to which factors like the pre-determined limitation of functions, lack of resources, and the use of personnel unskilled in recognising counselling need, have contributed to this assertion was impossible to assess. Anecdotal evidence suggested that educational counselling is very productive, leading to a satisfactory outcome for enquirer, providing institution and counsellor alike. On the other hand, this may be equally the case with information and advice enquiries, but follow-ups are much less likely to be made. However, the relative weight given to the functions of educational guidance may change as the clientele changes. Counselling appears to be assuming greater importance as services find themselves dealing with greater numbers of unemployed persons, for whom alternatives may be very limited and who may find great difficulty in accommodating themselves to their new circumstances.

Implementation

Implementation, that range of activities intended to ease the learner's pursuit of the agreed educational goal, is a hallmark of the new concept of educational guidance. Apart from advocacy, implementation also comprises coping activities and feedback. Coping activities take two main forms. The first is helping clients learn to deal with the institutions and agencies they come into contact with in an appropriate and effective way. At its simplest level, this may mean showing how to complete application forms, but it extends to teaching the client how to initiate change in provision, e.g. making a complaint about a tutor. The second form of coping is helping the client learn to deal with the educational demands of a chosen course of study. This may include help with study techniques or guidance on pre-entry learning, for example. Feedback may be defined as the discernment of patterns of need from the client, based on the systematic collection of data, and the presentation of this information to the providing institutions. Implied is the necessity of working with providers to effect changes in resource allocation, programme profiles, class times and so on. Occasionally, where institutions are unable or unwilling to provide a class, the Service will make its own provision.

Coping activity appears to be a function most commonly found with centre-type Services and particularly those targeted primarily at disadvantaged groups. For many other Services, this activity appears to be little in demand, with Services reporting that they provided such assistance where the client appeared to need it. Advocacy and feedback are sometimes contentious issues, which appear clearly to mark the division between those Services with a strong community-action orientation (usually of the centre-type, in 'neutral' premises and with a high degree of financial autonomy) and those which adopt a more traditional approach. In practice, there is no doubt that some of the Services which treat advocacy and feedback with caution do so through concern not to disrupt sometimes fragile relationships with sponsors and/or links. The question of these forms of implementation is also debated on principle. Some Services consider advocacy inappropriate; self-directed pursuit of an educational goal sorts the determined client from the half-hearted. Others view it as an inevitable extension of the guidance process. The same factors which caused clients to seek help at the first stage, exploration, will also cause them to need help at the second, implementation. For some Services, the greater the degree of educational disadvantage, the more the client needs advocacy at the implementation stage. Furthermore, they argue that if access to many continuing education opportunities is closed to adults, for whatever reasons, then they have an obligation to represent the potential consumer's view — in a way that will effect change in the allocation of resources. Individuals are unlikely to be able to do this for themselves; they need an agency which can approach providers on equal terms.

Even for those Services committed to implementation, both amount and type vary substantially. This function also demands resources, such as clerical help and professionals' time to establish and nurture the necessary contacts. For example, feedback involves three types of operation: keeping records of the numbers and types of enquiries; following up clients; and collating evidence of client need, to negotiate for change in provision where appropriate. While in theory it is here that Services have a crucial development role, in making coherent and amplifying the voice of the consumer, in practice feedback activity is limited. Nevertheless, there have been examples of negotiated change, often accomplished by force of personality, persuasive diplomacy and pulling strings. In such circumstances, the value of the Services' network of contacts and their advisory committees, often representative of the major institutions in the locality, may be inestimable.

PART 2: CASE STUDIES

CHAPTER 4

AIMS, METHODOLOGY AND CONDUCT OF THE CASE STUDY RESEARCH

Introduction
The Project's exploratory fieldwork provided a national perspective on independent educational guidance for adults and a broadly-applicable analytical framework. What we could not gauge were the strengths and weaknesses of each model and the emphasis of practice at the level of service to the client. We also found that almost all our informants lacked evidence of the impact of the guidance provided on their clientele. In other words, the consumer's viewpoint was noticeably absent; yet without it, any proposals which the Project might make for the development of educational guidance would be insecurely based. These considerations fundamentally informed the next phase of our research.

Aims and methodology
Our aims, broadly, were to consider the process of educational guidance from the point of view of the staff providing it; to consider this process also from the point of view of their clients; and to propose from the analysis appropriate areas for the development of practice.

These broad aims clearly suggested a case-study approach. Our limited time and staffing resources required the research to be concentrated on four Services. Since Services may be as readily characterised by location, staffing, orientation or funding as by structure, it was impossible to choose four which were fully representative of EGSA practice nationally. (Choice was also limited to Services which represented a variety of relationships with the public library service: see Chapter 1). However, we aimed to represent as far as possible the diversity of provision and practice. The four Services consequently selected were:

Service A, essentially of the link-chain type, but converting to a link-chain-centre. This Service was manned by volunteers, who offered a once-weekly session at central premises provided by the local Careers Service, which also gave other back-up facilities. Service A was understood to offer information, advice and referral.

Service B, a centre-type Service, was converting from all-volunteer to mixed staffing with the recent appointment of a temporary full-time coordinator. The EGSA also employed part-time clerical help and was located in the central branch of a public library, which provided back-up facilities. This EGSA was understood to place particular emphasis on counselling.

Service C, a link-chain-centre Service, employed one and a half full-time non-professional staff on temporary contracts. It was located in 'neutral', fairly central premises (actually owned by the local polytechnic) and was undorotood to havo active cupport from a wide range of continuing education institutions in the area, not least in the systems of 'links' developed. This EGSA was understood to place particular emphasis on information provision and assisted referral. Unlike the other Services selected, its normal mode of client contact was by telephone rather than by personal visits.

Service D, a centre-type Service, was manned by two full-time permanent, professional staff and one part-time secretary. It was located in 'neutral' high street premises and was understood to place particular emphasis on implementation activity, especially advocacy.

Our exploratory interviews had suggested that the pattern of demand varied according to the time of year. To allow for this and produce a more complete picture, we allocated different times of the year for our research at each Service. This allocation was made on a random basis, since we had no evidence to suggest that any one Service performed better or worse at particular times of the year. The date allocation for each Service was:
Service A: July/August 1981;
Service B: November 1981;
Service C: December 1981/January 1982;
Service D: March 1982.
Our decision to investigate educational guidance as an interactive process between guidance worker and client suggested that we could study only a relatively small number of cases from each Service. However, we considered that this approach offered many advantages — particularly in providing both parties with the opportunity to reflect in detail and depth on their perceptions of the process in which they were engaged. We decided therefore on a target of twenty clients to be drawn from each Service, a total of eighty. In this way, we hoped to provide a holistic picture of educational guidance in a variety of EGSA settings, which might have a general applicability.

Objectives and data assembly
The aims and approach outlined in the last section are here broken down into practical objectives, accompanied by explanation of the method of data collection. The detailed method of fieldwork is described in the next section.

A. *Description of the educational information resources of each Service* was intended to discover the extent and nature of the information base and its adequacy to meet enquiries received. It was to be achieved by examination of the Service's stock of literature and through tape-recorded interviews with guidance workers.

B. *Analyses of the numbers and kinds of educational enquiries received* were to be sought from each Service to provide context to the Project's caseloads. These data were understood to be available from the Services' own Reports.

C. *Analysis of the kinds of people making enquiries* was intended to provide a limited picture of those attracted to use EGSAs for educational guidance. It was to be achieved by gathering personal data in questionnaire form from clients from our sample, with most attention concentrated on their educational background and activities. (The questionnaire is reproduced in Appendix 2a).

D. *Analysis of the responses given by the guidance worker (i.e. the range and type of help offered to the client)* was at the heart of the research and was to be elicited in two ways. First, EGSA staff were to be asked to record their understanding of the nature of each enquiry and the actions they took on a simple record form to be completed immediately after the transaction of the enquiry. (The record form is reproduced in Appendix 2b). Second, each worker dealing with a client taking part in the research was to be interviewed on the conduct of the particular enquiry, under the broad headings of information, assessment, advice, counselling and implementation. This interview schedule (reproduced in Appendix 2c) was to be administered in an open-ended way, allowing staff to digress from the order of questions where appropriate and permitting wider comment based on practice and experience where relevant.

E. *Evaluation of the transaction from the point of view of the guidance worker* was to be made in order to compare workers' and clients' levels of satisfaction on the conduct of the enquiry. After the interview described in D above, staff were asked to rate the five components of the transaction, where applicable, on a scale from 0-10: 0 being the least good and 10 the best. The ratings scale is reproduced in Appendix 2d.

F. *Analysis of the responses given (i.e. the range and type of help offered from the point of view of the client)* was considered of equal importance to the interviewing of EGSA staff and was to be administered in the same way. It observed the same broad headings, but was also concerned to elicit the fullest information on the context in which the enquiry was made. It is reproduced in Appendix 2e.

G. *Evaluation of the transaction from the point of view of the client* was to be made for purposes of comparison with guidance workers' evaluations, and by the same method. The ratings scale is reproduced in Appendix 2f.

H. *Follow-up of clients* was designed to determine actual as opposed to envisaged outcome. Where possible, clients were to be telephoned and asked how far they had pursued what they had intended at the time of interview; where clients were not on the telephone, then follow-up letters would be sent.

I. *Supplementary information* on the Service's background, operations, and relations with other agencies was to be gathered through interviews with key personnel and examination of relevant documents, such as the Service's Annual Reports.

Conduct of the fieldwork
The research approach and detailed methodology were piloted at Service A and proved generally satisfactory. In view of the relative complexity of the research design and the concepts underlying it, the appointed fieldworkers needed both initial and continued supportive briefing; this was given on a group and individual basis. Additionally, each fieldworker spent some time before the allotted research period in familiarising herself with the Project's earlier work and with the operation of the particular Service. This included reviewing the Service's published and unpublished reports and preliminary interviewing of Service personnel. Service C's fieldworker was offered, and accepted, an invitation to attend its Steering Committee meetings and weekly case reviews.

The standard approach procedure was as follows. Each fieldworker briefed the guidance workers concerned on the purpose of the research, using a standardised format, and invited their cooperation. They were asked to complete the interview record form immediately after interviewing a client and to be available for main interviewing as soon as practicable afterwards. They were also asked to act as intermediaries between clients and the Project by explaining the purposes of the research and inviting their cooperation. They were asked not to be selective in any way, but to invite clients' assistance chronologically as they used the Service. Thus introduced, the field workers assumed responsibility for explaining the purpose of the research to clients and for seeking their cooperation. Clients accepting the Project's invitation were interviewed as soon as possible, away from the Service's immediate premises, most usually at home. After interview, clients' permission to follow-up at an appropriate later date was also sought.

Minor practical variations were to be expected, in view of the different organisation of the four Services. These variations are outlined below:

A. There were a few occasions arising with all four Services, when, largely because of pressure of work, guidance workers did not complete the interview record form until some hours after the relevant client interview. This resulted in some loss of detail, but not significantly so.

B. Except on a very few occasions, when the guidance worker had unavoidable prior commitments, interviewing on their perceptions of the transaction with the client was held within one day of the client contact. The length of these tape-recorded interviews varied enormously, from fifteen minutes to over two hours. Where a worker had dealt with more than one client, the subsequent interviews were considerably shorter than the first, since much of the first interview was given over to more general discussion of the worker's approach, attitudes and perceptions of her/his role. There were many occasions when guidance workers gave generously of their free time to complete this section of data-gathering. The ratings-scales on evaluation of such client contact appeared to work well (except for reservations about the distinctions drawn between the advice and counselling functions of educational guidance).

C. Services A and B were manned primarily by volunteers working on a rota basis. Exigencies of timetabling meant that, at the times allocated for the research at these Services, one volunteer's activities would be greatly over-represented. It was felt that this feature might distort the general picture of Services A and B's guidance approach and steps were taken to obtain a wider spread of EGSA worker/client interactions, largely by extending the time-span of the research.

D. At Service C, there was some reluctance among personnel to ask clients for their cooperation in the research, partly from concern for the confidentiality of the consultations and partly because the Service operated very largely by telephone contact (of the twenty main interviews carried out, sixteen were based on telephone contact only with the office). It was felt to be inappropriate at the end of what was often a brief, anonymous conversation to explain the research procedure and to invite participation. So the fieldworker agreed to make that initial approach for herself, (by telephone or letter within forty-eight hours, or immediately in the case of personal visitors). This meant that clients had to be introduced to the research by a hitherto anonymous research worker. It was seen to be important by the fieldworker and the Chairman of the Steering Committee to demonstrate the integrity of the research relationship by enclosing a covering letter from the Chairman and a fieldworker's identity card with the confirmation of the interview appointment.

E. There was no difficulty in enlisting the cooperation of clients. The fieldworkers recorded a total of only three refusals. However, a few clients at Service C were 'lost' when they preferred to give no name. Twenty clients each were recruited from Services A, B, C. At Service D, however, pressure of time meant that the Project was able to recruit sixteen clients only, a shortfall of four. Thus the total number of clients interviewed was seventy-six.

F. Almost all clients were interviewed within a short time of their visit to the Service. The majority of these interviews were conducted at the client's home; a minority were held on premises away from the Service's immediate premises, where clients considered such an arrangement more convenient. As with the guidance workers, interviews were tape-recorded (a procedure which caused only the smallest inhibition in a few cases) and varied substantially in length. The fieldworkers found almost all these interviewees remarkably trusting and forthcoming, with a wealth of information and reflection. Most seemed flattered that anyone should be prepared to attend to their points of view in such detail. Indeed, this aspect of the interviews resulted in the only real problem experienced by the fieldworkers, that they were occasionally seen by clients as a further resource for information and guidance. It seemed quite unethical in some cases not to respond in general terms to requests for further direction. Clients also accepted the questionnaire and ratings scales very well (although again there were difficulties over the distinction between advice and counselling).

G. All clients readily agreed to be contacted again for follow-up; and this exercise was achieved largely without difficulty. A small minority did not respond; mainly those clients who were not on the telephone and did not reply to fieldworkers' letters. Some were understood to have moved out of the area.

H. Supplementary information was gathered through interviews with persons identified by the guidance workers as making an important contribution to the work of the Service. Fieldworkers were also provided with published (and some unpublished) information about the Service.

In all, the data gathered took three main forms: information from clients' questionnaires; the ratings given to elements of the transaction by guidance workers and by clients; the interviews with guidance workers and clients. The last represented a considerable data analysis task, consisting as it did of nearly 200 interviews. Transcripts of all these interviews were made and the more factual incidents (e.g. number of options discussed) were translated onto prepared data analysis forms for later tabulation. This process caused individual fieldworkers some concern, since there were inevitable simplifications of very complex material. More importantly, there were occasions when the judgments involved were essentially subjective. Our problem was exacerbated because there had been considerable resistance from guidance workers to our *original* proposal that the interview between *worker and client* be tape-recorded. Objections were made primarily on the grounds that the use of a tape-recorder would intrude on the confidentiality of the interview, although there were also technical difficulties in the case of Service C. So, despite cross-checking of the ascriptions made to the data sheets, there were occasions when the final decision was based on the personal judgment of the fieldworker. We feel, however, that the margin of error is small and does not affect the findings overall. We profited enormously from the great strength of the interview methodology, namely the unique richness of comment on more intangible matters — process, values, understanding, perceptions — which in our opinion were emphatically well portrayed through this method.

A separate report was prepared on each Service and its clients and this was circulated for comment to the Services involved in the case-study fieldwork. The findings which follow represent an amalgamation of those four reports.

CHAPTER 5
THE FOUR EGSAs

Introduction
This chapter provides a descriptive account of each of the four Services participating in the research. Their inception, aims, funding, management, staffing, location and operation are considered, as are the particular successes and problems which were drawn to our attention or which were apparent in our discussions with key informants.

Service A
Service A is located in a northern city which is bounded mainly by rural hinterland. Its traditional industries have been in decline for many years. It is well-served with continuing education institutions, including a university, a college of higher education and a college of further education, though in recent years the city attracted publicity by suspending LEA adult education classes entirely for a period.

The genesis of Service A was in 1978, with the coincidence of two related events. One was that the research experience of a member of staff of the adult education department of City A's university had led him to a conviction that:

> ...access involved information and advice. It's not purely a question of admission requirements...because of the proliferation of post-school education and training, really there was a need for some kind of central Service which would synthesise that kind of information and provide a basis for choice for people.

As a consequence, he wrote and published *Beyond School*, a short and simply written guide to post-school education and training opportunities in City A, which was distributed widely throughout the city and sold for ten pence per copy. At the same time, and quite independently, the local Adult Education Coordinating Committee was considering the need for some sort of guidance service. *Beyond School*'s author was invited by the Committee to set up a working party, under the Committee's aegis, to consider the possibilities of creating a Service. It is this working party, informally constituted and effectively autonomous of the Committee, which has since been responsible for coordinating Service A's development and activity. Invitations to membership were extended to a wide range of education and training providers in the area, as well as to those with related interests, such as the public library service and CAB. However, those most active on the working party appear in the main to have come from continuing education. The Committee's attendance was said to consist of up to twelve people, of whom five were identified as 'very committed' to Service A.

In brief, Service A's aim is to provide 'basic information and advice to ANY adults about ANY educational or training opportunities' in City A (their emphasis). A note in a subsequent edition of *Beyond School* provides more detail of its initial form:

> ...(Service A) is run jointly by all the agencies and institutions which are involved with education and training beyond the end of compulsory school, and its aim is to help would-be adult students to find the courses which might suit them and also to give them more general information and advice. As well as this booklet, (Service A) produces a series of free information leaflets...about particular kinds of courses and opportunities. In addition, (Service A) holds regular, open counselling days...which are advertised in the local press. These usually take place at the beginning of September and the beginning of March. *Anyone* over sixteen, with *any* kind of educational, training or career question or problems is welcome to drop in, and we will do what we can to help.

From its inception, Service A has seen itself essentially as a link-chain or network type of Service. There were two main reasons for this. The first relates to the perceived nature of educational information:

> ...We didn't feel that we could centralize — even with all the money, you know, in the world — we didn't feel that we could centralize information about courses and opportunities because a lot of that is very soft information in the sense that it's very difficult to put down on paper — it's coal-face information — you actually need to go and talk to somebody — and it shifts — it's fluid — I don't think we've ever felt that a kind of centralized shop or whatever was on because I think it is in the nature of educational information that you have to go pretty soon to the coal-face to get it, and I think that'll always be so because I think so much of what goes on in education and so much to do with courses is actually tacit or implicit rather than explicit, and you can't actually get it down in hard form...

The second reason for selecting the link-chain model was the low level of finance required, with consequent implications for the durability of the Service:

> ...The more centralized your Service, the more obvious a target it is for cuts. The more you're sort of embedded or can subtly draw on institutional resources, the more difficult it is to cut the thing. We're very aware of cuts.

However, the advantages of a central point for the Service were recognised. Indeed, there had initially been the possibility of obtaining a full-time temporary MSC appointment for the project, which was thwarted because of cutbacks. On the other hand, there was also the feeling that:

> ...it was a blessing in disguise actually, because it forced us again onto this network idea, and if we'd got a STEP worker we might have got very used to having a STEP worker and become lazy and built the whole thing round one person.

There were still psychological and political reasons for Service A to have a public, central presence and for that centre to be located in 'neutral' premises. Service A were fortunate in having as their representative from the local Careers Service an individual with a long-standing commitment to adult educational guidance. He was able to offer the Service some valuable back-up facilities.

From March 1980 to February 1981, Service A moved into its first operational phase, with three main areas of activity. The first was an expansion of the information approach in *Beyond School,* to include a series of leaflets on various types of provision in the city (e.g. basic education; vocational education; part-time degrees; courses on social work). These leaflets (as well as *Beyond School*) were distributed at various points in the city. They included an invitation to contact Service A at the local Careers Office for further help. This was the second development. The Careers Office information officer agreed to act as information distributor and referral point for the Service. Thirdly, the Service organised two collaboratively-staffed Open Days at a city centre location. The first attracted over a hundred callers, but the second, perhaps because of mishandled publicity, only ten. However, in all the Service recorded about 350 clients during this first year.

Even with this modest level of activity, there were difficulties in dealing with many clients which appeared to be most keenly felt by the Careers Service information officer. While 'about half' had apparently straightforward information-only requests, which could be dealt with by using the extensive collection of materials, the remainder presented the information officer with considerable difficulties. For those clients who appeared to need referral, it was hard to contact and arrange appointments, even with those continuing educators most firmly committed to Service A. Referral to distant and anonymous departments was thought likely to incur drop-out. Moreover, many clients appeared to present counselling need, and it was these people for whom the information officer, herself untrained in counselling skills, felt most concern:

> ...I've only ever worked with young people up to the age of eighteen, and I think, especially if you've been a teacher — you can cut off conversations, you can angle conversations your way — but I find with adults, particularly in City A at the moment, their stories are so utterly depressing, and they come in, and they've been from pillar to post already — most of them, they've got very sad stories to tell — especially we get young men between the ages of 30 and 40, they've got mortgages, kids, and it's their second redundancy, and I can't just brightly say 'Oh well, take this sheet on correspondence colleges and we'll fix you up with an interview later'.

With the Careers Service's own adult guidance capacity already overstretched, such clients might spend up to half-an-hour talking to the information officer, though, as she commented, 'I think most of them know that all I'm doing is listening'.

These circumstances led the information officer to suggest a solution to Service A:

40

...It just struck me that it might be useful to try and use the centre for some kind of appointment system and in-depth interviewing, which I myself do not do. I don't give vocational guidance, and I find that with adults it's very difficult not to. It would be very useful to me if I could have some appointment times that I could give people when they could come back and actually talk in depth to a counsellor — and obviously for me it's going to be great if I can have them on site — so I suggested that then — it seemed to come as a bombshell.

It was the adoption of this scheme which marked Service A's second developmental stage. This was a direct-service advisory session held at the Careers Office, from 3.30 to 6.30 each Tuesday, through eleven months of the year, by appointment made via the information officer or on a drop-in basis. Volunteers to man this provision were recruited from the working party and their contacts. Nearly all were professionally employed in continuing education. A team of approximately ten undertook a short five-afternoons training programme, consisting of sessions on counselling, information services, and familiarisation with the range of relevant provision in the city. The main criterion of a volunteer's acceptability was seen to be her or his ability to 'relate to the very wide variety of people who are likely to come in;' the final judgment on this matter was in the hands of the training organiser. This phase of the Service's activity came into operation in mid 1981, with one volunteer (called an adviser) in attendance per three-hour session, on a rota basis. Clients, who were most likely to have made an appointment, were greeted by the information officer and could browse in the library if they had to wait, or after their interview. Interviews were held in an office vacated by Careers staff for the afternoon, and were booked for half-an-hour. The minority of clients who dropped in might receive briefer assistance or be invited to make an appointment for the following week. The Service was already becoming busier; between April and July 1981 it dealt with at least 200 clients, though only a minority were seen by the volunteers. There was no 'follow-up' policy and few clients were understood to make second visits.

From the evidence presented to us, it appeared that Service A was still faced with a number of unresolved issues for its current operation and future development. These were:

A. While the Service had clearly achieved considerable progress in developing a useful network of contacts, there were problems in its referral procedure. Named contacts might be difficult to find when needed spontaneously. And the Service had not yet achieved a comprehensive coverage. This was partly because some institutions were so devolved within themselves that there was no key contact; but it was also due to a plain lack of cooperation on the part of some providers and an acknowledged lack of vigour on Service A's part. Clients were known sometimes to be given 'an incredible run-around'.

41

Such deficiencies appeared likely to have serious implications for a Service placing such reliance on referral for detailed information and advice.

B. There was also substantial divergence of opinion on the place of information in Service A's work. For some advisers, the basic information given in the Service's booklet and leaflets (as well as access to the Careers Service's library) was considered sufficient. Others were more doubtful. One adviser, for example, spoke of the difficulties arising from having to deal with clients on the basis of last year's brochures and expressed concern about her own grasp of provision. She commented:

> ...I'm very much in the position of learning myself...really for assisting in a browsing capacity than acting as an adviser.

Another remarked:

> ...We may well be forgiven for not spotting that someone's marriage is breaking down; we certainly won't be forgiven for giving them the wrong information.

Another area of potential difficulty was that the Service's own information was concentrated almost entirely on provision within the city boundaries (understandably in view of its limited resources), but this was seen as in many ways an artificial division. Additionally, the Careers Service library back-up, although considered extremely valuable, was identified by the information officer as presenting problems. It was almost entirely geared to school-leavers and was said in some areas of education and training to offer less good coverage than the public library, to whom clients were sometimes referred.*

C. Similar divergence of opinion appeared in the weight apparently given by individual advisers to advice, counselling and referral. One adviser might see the interaction as essentially informational, and another emphasise counselling. Some advisers were understood to use referral much more than others. (Monitoring of advisers' actions was not conducted by Service A).

D. Facilitating access to education for the disadvantaged might demand the direction of very limited resources into deliberate strategies to reach such groups, and thus away from the Service's 'general responsibility'. The Service had decided on a policy whereby:

> ...We make no distinction in terms of the level of need of people coming in, whether they're looking for basic education or something more exalted.

However, two outreach approaches to peripheral housing estates were under consideration, one using branch libraries and the other the community education bus.

E. Such exercises might well have the effect of increasing the numbers of clients approaching Service A, as might increased public-

---

*Service A's relationship with its public library service is considered in detail in the Project's Report to the British Library.

ity. However, both from the point of view of the Careers Service back-up and from the increased demands likely to be made on the volunteers, expansion on a rapid scale was not feasilble. At the same time, Service A was clearly concerned to demonstrate the extent of demand to providing institutions in the city. Service A's finances were insecure. 'It's not so much hand-to-mouth as sometimes this hand and sometimes the other' — and many of its costs 'hidden' (that is, absorbed by sympathetic institutions), again a system with considerable insecurities. Those institutions reluctant to offer financial support might be more ready to do so when presented with evidence of substantial demand, such as numbers of clients using the Service, and particularly, numbers referred to each institution. It was envisaged that Service A might be able to exert pressure on uncooperative institutions:

> ...I think there may come a point where we've been around long enough and we've got enough climate of support for us to be able to come back to institutions and say, 'Look we want a regular contribution and if you don't, you either buy in or you buy out — or you stay out'.

F. Such considerations were instrumental in Service A's decision systematically to log and analyse its enquiries, from the second phase of its development. However, in the short term at least, it was considered that such a strategy was unlikely to be effective, since there was often over-demand for educational and training facilities in the city. The Service's potential for student recruitment lacked relevance when courses were already over-subscribed. On the other hand, there were areas of provision where competition for students was already very apparent and where, as a consequence, some of Service A's working party saw a strong case for 'as it were, being on the side...of the enquirer'.

Service A was in an early developmental stage and consequently still defining its role, strategies and practice at the time of our research. It had survived for nearly two years and expanded its operations on a budget of a few hundred pounds and generously 'hidden' funding. During this time it had also established the beginnings of cooperation between providers and introduced the notion of more client-centred guidance. As one adviser commented, 'At least our information from the word "go" points to multiple possibilities'. The great sense of commitment to Service A felt by its advocates was summed up by one thus:

> ...We don't have the assurances of continuity and the norms and the rules and the support and the money that institutions have but, on the other hand, there's the spark there, I think, which you very often don't get in the institutional mould — all the people who are centrally involved in it are involved because they believe in the thing. I know that sounds sort of maybe a bit corny, but we all of us are very busy people and we're all of us doing this basically because we believe in it.

Service B

Service B is located in a city which is part of a densely-populated conurbation. Its traditional industry has been in decline for many years and it has a large immigrant population. The city is well-provided with educational institutions, including a university and one of the ten largest community colleges in the country, responsible for organising a huge variety of courses at all levels. A nearby city is also well-served with a wide variety of provision, including a university and a polytechnic.

The development of Service B dates from 1976, when the Local Development Council for Adult Education (LDCAE) set up a working group on advisory and counselling services for continuing education. Its first report, produced in 1977, gave evidence of the need for a local advisory service:

> ...which should develop a client-centred approach and encourage advisors whose loyalty would be to their local community and the needs of individuals rather than to any particular institution.

By mid-1978, and following discussion between the LDCAE and the further education officer, the scheme envisaged by what was now a steering group was a computer-assisted information, advice and counselling service, located in the central library of City B's public library service:

> ...since mid-1978 a steering group of the Local Development Council, consisting of representatives of the Standing Academic Planning Board, the Careers Service, the LEA, and the Open University, together with the chief librarian, have been formulating proposals which will lead to a project whose primary aims will be to provide information for educational establishments in City B about the nature and range of enquiries about educational opportunities in the Metropolitan area; to test the effectiveness of and the relevance of a computer data-base which has, implicit in its structure, a 'browsing' facility; and to test our basic hypothesis that the central library/local library network is of key importance to the establishment and development of an advisory service, which can refer onwards, to educational and social providers, and inwards from them, to the Advisory Centre.[33]

This scheme, which was costed at nearly £30,000 per year and included the employment of five full-time staff, did not attract the necessary funding. In July 1979 it was decided to go ahead with a smaller-scale Service, since accommodation was promised by the library and some pump-priming funds were available from the Open University, the local university extra-mural department and, later, from the LEA. The OU was also interested in supporting the computerised information element of Service B, as was the British Library.

Preparations for opening the Service began almost immediately. An early-retired college lecturer was appointed co-ordinator and two others as advisers (called counsellors). All were part-time voluntary appointments, paid expenses only. From October to December 1979 this core team, all experienced continuing educators, pursued their own self-training programme, described as 'more or less an ad hoc programme according to our needs'. It included meetings with key informants such as Careers Service personnel and individuals with professional counselling training, as well as meetings between the three to discuss 'hopes, doubts, fears, limitations and so on', which, despite the cumulative experience of the three, were considerable:

...I don't think it would be true to say that we were bursting over with confidence and security because first of all, the — what one might call the information side — the amount of information which one must not so much know, as know where to find, is tremendous. I think we all felt that the first people who came in might come in with queries about something with which we were completely and utterly ignorant — that's one side of it. The other side, which people feel to a different extent and in different ways, which is a sort of personal matter — is what you might call the counselling proper...Although we've all had experience in this in other spheres, with a completely open door policy I suppose we were dubious, doubtful, worried, concerned, about what might face us with the first enquirers, so I think a training programme — a training period — is very necessary.

At the same time, the co-ordinator was engaged in a series of preparatory meetings with educational and related providers in the city.

The Service opened to the public in January 1980. It was located in an office in the central library; a part-time clerk was appointed at the same time to provide secretarial and administrative support. An educational guidance service which was firmly integrated with its public library service had been envisaged to offer great benefits to both parties, as well as to clients:

...The service could be available for sixty-eight hours per week if necessary (i.e. full library open hours).

The chief librarian and his staff, through the nature of the library services, have considerable professional expertise in the recording and retrieval of information on public demand.

The central library is linked to branch libraries throughout the district. Such a network would ensure the possibility of *local* 'first contact' enquiries which could be fed to the central agency. The same convenience of opening hours would apply to the branches.

Library staff would have to be specifically trained as receptionists. This, of course, is not to imply that they do not know already how to treat members of the public, or how to handle information. It is simply that some emphasis would have to be laid on the fact that even the most casual sounding enquiry about educational opportunities may stem from a deeply felt personal need. Adults lacking in self-confidence or the ability to articulate precise requests may be put off by a formal, impersonal response.

A number of quite complicated arrangements were agreed, to ensure that both clients who had come to the central library specifical-

45

ly to consult Service B and those who were identified by staff in the library's several departments as likely to benefit from consultation, were directed to it. The library's staff would continue to act as information providers, but any client perceived to be in need of information which could not be provided from the library's resources, or of advice or counselling, was to be referred to the ground-floor Enquiry Desk. The Desk's staff undertook responsibility to arrange an appointment with Service B. At this point clients were asked for *basic* information about their enquiry. This procedure served two functions. First, it ensured that the client was indeed best referred to Service B. Second it allowed the Service's counsellor to prepare for the interview. By maintaining duplicate diaries through liaison with the Service's clerk, the library thus provided a full-time appointments system, to link clients into the part-time counsellors' availability.

Service B was at the same time expanding its operations in several important ways. The first of these was an increase in the number of counsellors. The potential of experienced individuals, widely-drawn from the community, had been accepted from the beginning, both to enable more clients to benefit from the Service and to take the Service into the community and reach those who for geographical or social reasons did not use the central library. A volunteer recruitment meeting was arranged in February 1980. A short article in the local newspapers failed to attract response, but a number of 'word-of-mouth' contacts did attend and volunteer their services. Three were university employees; one was a schools' liaison officer; there was an information officer and a lecturer in psychology. Four were mature students. One was an OU tutor-counsellor and another an industrial training officer. Training sessions numbered ten, between March and July 1980, and included introductory talks by a careers officer, the chief librarian and the training officer from Social Services. Other sessions were taken by the three counsellors and included case studies, role-playing, an introduction to some local 'access' courses and general feedback sessions. Trainee counsellors were also invited to sit-in during client interviews. They started counselling in August: their own sessions were not monitored, but new counsellors arranged to meet as a group to discuss any problems they encountered. Between August and December 1980 seven of these recruits had seen clients. Four were working on a regular basis, seeing one or two clients per week; the others had counselled on an ad hoc basis, deputising for absent counsellors.

The second development during this period was the computerisation of some of the Service's information. The British Library provided funding for this project, whose purpose was 'to explore an experimental, small scale, local scheme for the provision of a computer-assisted data bank of information on educational opportunities which could be used to support the work of an Education Advice Service', and its result 'a model data base, available "on line" in City B via a telephone link connected to the Open University computer at the Regional Open University Centre'. This project ran from May to December 1980 and was collaboratively devised by City B central library staff, the Open University and Service B. Although successful in its own terms, and despite the considerable national (and international) interest it aroused, the data-bank which resulted was never used by the Service. There were two principal problems. First, the file content was limited. Although some 750 courses were described, they were entirely those available at the four major colleges in the LEA area (not a particularly useful geographical criterion for Service B), much of their part-time provision was excluded, and the information that was included was limited to what could be obtained from descriptions in brochures. Second, there was no guaranteed commitment to up-dating. In a report on the project, it was noted that 'although the file structure may remain serviceable, the information contained, unless up-dated, soon becomes useless. The irony is that having created an instrument, a main characteristic of which is the facility for continuous correction, we are unable to take proper advantage of that facility'.

The third development during this phase was an increasing attention to outreach, not only in introducing Service B to more providers, but also in moving out to general and specific client groups. Ventures included an 'open day', held in a nearby shopping centre; information and advice-giving sessions on the library's peripatetic bus; and a leafleting of employers giving them information on the ways in which Service B might help workers about to be made redundant. These exercises met with varying degrees of response.

By mid-1981, Service B was under some pressure from its steering group, because of an apparent lack of success on a quantifiable basis. The Service was offering guidance to some 250 people annually; some of the volunteer team had dropped out. The LDCAE requested evidence of what the Service was actually accomplishing. It was decided to appoint a paid co-ordinator for a short period, to determine whether some well co-ordinated publicity initiatives could increase the use of the Service and justify a substantial grant from the LEA, for Service B to consolidate its work during 1982-3. The local authority granted a further £3,500, and the paid co-ordinator began work in October 1981. This period was marked by a large increase in client numbers, largely through the successful use of local radio and other outreach initiatives. The EGSA dealt with 406 enquiries over a three and a half month period. The volunteer team was expanded, and a further training programme anticipated an increase from six to twenty counsellors by the end of March 1982.

Our research took place during the early part of this second phase of Service B's development and examined its work from the central library base. At that time, the Service occupied a small office on the fourth floor. The room had two telephones (internal and external), two armchairs, one typist chair and two desks. Information was stored in boxes on bookshelves. A client making an initial approach to Service B would telephone or call personally to the central library and ask for the Service directly, or to be referred there by library staff. The clerical assistant was present between 10.00 am and 1.30 pm to give information or make appointments to see counsellors. After 1.30 pm and up to 8.00 pm clients made an appointment through the library's ground floor Enquiry Desk, which kept a duplicate diary. When keeping an appointment, clients were asked to approach the Enquiry Desk for instructions. The Desk staff then telephoned the counsellor on duty to say that the client had arrived. The client was directed to the third floor to be met and taken to the fourth floor up a private staircase (there was no direct access to this floor, since it had been closed to the public for some time). If the clerical assistant was present she removed herself, work and typewriter to a desk outside the office. Counselling sessions varied in length between one and a half hours and ten minutes: the average session was three-quarters of an hour to an hour. After the session a form was normally filled in, giving details of the client. There was no specific policy of 'follow-up' of clients and few clients made a second visit.

Our discussions with key informants illuminated some central and unresolved conflicts in several areas of Service B's operations. These are considered below.

A. Service B's relationship with its host, the central library, was in some respects a very uneasy one. A major difficulty lay in convincing hard-pressed, expert information-oriented librarians of the validity of the work which Service B did. As one librarian commented:

> ...many staff feel that it's a bit of an irrelevance — that the information's here and that we provide it — we do it much more efficiently than they do. There's rather a lot of 'us' and 'they' about it. It's just a completely different sort of ball-game they're in — we can't easily relate to it...it seems to be putting a lot of money into a service which, in fact, helps very few people. When the Service B people say, 'Oh, we've had a heavy day today — I've seen three people' we just laugh to the limits — I mean, we just say, 'Well, I've had thirty in the last hour' and there's no sort of common ground — it's the difference between counselling and information provision — but we get very sort of — I don't know — scornful of this sort of approach.

The central library obviously had no wish to give over its own educational information role, and this had a number of important effects on Service B. First, it did not benefit numerically from the great number of 'information only' enquiries which boost many EGSAs' client-contact figures. Second, it skewed Service B's orientation firmly towards advice and counselling. Thirdly, such 'information only' enquiries as were directed to Service B by library staff were complex ones which library staff were unable to deal with themselves.

In fact, with the exception of the Enquiry Desk, library departments generally did not refer clients to the EGSA. Many staff, particularly those at junior level, had only the vaguest notions of Service B's functions and none had visited its office. The Service itself had offered library staff only an introductory briefing session, so that at the time of our research most staff had had no contact with the Service for nearly two years. This was a factor of great importance in reducing referrals, or, in the case of the Enquiry Desk, in making sometimes inappropriate referrals, based on an inaccurate picture of Service B's functions. The problem was compounded by the far from public or visible location of the Service. Thus, the potentially fruitful relationship between an EGSA and a large, networked public library service, envisaged in the scheme's proposals, had not been adequately exploited.*

B. The problem that 'knowledge, understanding, procedures and so on don't percolate down as widely or as thoroughly or as sympathetically as they might', so evident in Service B's relationship with its host, was apparent with other institutions and agencies which the EGSA had identified as key contacts. Reliance on the steering group members to alert and sensitise their institutional colleagues to the Service was not an effective strategy where, for example, a staff of 500 was involved.

The Service was consequently engaged in a programme of promotional visits, sometimes with considerable success, sometimes less so. Within an institution, for example, one department might be much more sympathetic than another. Such outreach was characterised as 'a very long haul' by one of our informants. But it is apparent that this is a vital task, and one which requires not only active initiation but also continuous feedback. Such activity benefits the client as much as the Service, since it allows the opportunity for mutual briefing and more accurate referral. This was a matter of importance for Service B, since it was attempting to build up a network of named contacts who were more than in-depth information providers. It was envisaged that they should have the ability 'to recognise that a person has aspirations which, to begin with, were probably somewhat vague and not based on a full appraisal of the situation — to recognise that they have taken the first step of discussing with a sympathetic and informed person their own aspirations in the light of their own situation and that it would then be a question of the second stage — discussing with the client a particular course or courses of action.' It was not Service B's policy to refer all clients on, but emphasis was given in volunteers' training to allowing them to develop an awareness of their own limitations and thus to refer on as it seemed appropriate and acceptable to the client.

---

*Service B's relationship with its public library service is considered in detail in the Project's Report to the British Library.

C. Volunteers had been envisaged from the Service's inception as an integral part of EGSA policy that it should use the great variety of skills and experience that the local community had to offer. There were also pragmatic advantages, with adequate funding so hard to secure. But the status and role of the volunteers caused conflict. The steering group had envisaged that the original core team of three should represent the 'professional' counselling face of Service B. This was soon not acceptable to the three, nor to the additional volunteers recruited, and the distinction was abandoned. The use of 'non-professionals' did, however, raise doubts about the quality of the Service offered. From the central library, for example, there was comment that:

> Educational advice is extraordinarily difficult — we realise this when we deal with the public — it is quite a specialist field and, from our point of view, the sheer complexity of the information...it may be a bit unfair to call them amateurish but the fact that they don't seem to have the up-to-date books, for example, makes me just wonder how up-to-date they are. It may be they're using the 'phone far more than we are, in which case it's probably not a problem but I just wonder.

At the same time, there was criticism from some of the steering group that the process of preparing volunteers for starting work was over-long, to the neglect of building up numbers of client contacts and of outreach, matters which are closely bound up with funding:

> ...I've been much criticised for the length of time that has been spent on the training of the counselling team. To be fair, there are others who say perhaps it's not been long enough but, I mean, the balance has been saying, you know, 'Why spend all this time on training the counselling team? Let's have results' and I think this is where the funding side has hit us so much — that people have been arguing — we've got funding for a limited period — if it is going to be renewed we must prove ourselves. The argument which will convince other people is a quantitative argument.

Service B was also seeking to resolve a number of organisational problems in the use of volunteers. They arose principally in the areas of referral procedure and record-keeping, where there were great difficulties in maintaining uniformity. There were problems in reaching agreement on conducting a monitoring exercise by telephone. There were counsellors who did not attend many training or group meetings. As a result, there was little agreement of views or approach within the counselling team:

> ...I would say among a proportion of the counselling team there is the beginning of a corporate spirit — very informal and loose but I think it's there — but I think there are others with whom this hasn't occurred yet.

At an individual level, volunteers interpreted their roles and commitment to the Service very variably. For example, while the Service generally had a positive policy towards advocacy, not all counsellors were agreed about acting in this way. Feedback was also undeveloped.

Service B is a complex and ambitious project which provides an interesting illustration of the advantages and disadvantages of collaborative management and funding. Despite the conflicts of interest and attitude in the Service, this approach also offered great strength. As the voluntary co-ordinator commented:

> ...In the whole question of funding, there are those who say the Service ought to be taken over by the LEA. Now, I'm wholly against that. I'm fully in favour of the LEA funding us more generously than it has done up to the moment but I think in my book it is absolutely essential that a Service of this nature retains its independence and its neutrality. The steering group — I mean, there are some who say, you know, 'We can't go on for ever with the steering group' and so on — to me, it's an essential; it's messy — I know one can argue it's a typically British ad hoc way of doing things but it does act, as it were, as a kind of buffer between the various establishments and the Service. If this Service was part of the LEA then I think it would be extremely inhibited. I mean, in a sense now, the conflicts and the battles — the disagreements — can to some extent be aired and, if not resolved, at any rate ventilated in a steering group situation but if, you know, whoever was in my role was an official of the LEA, I think this would be an impossible situation.

Service C

Service C is located in a city which is a regional business, shopping and leisure centre. It serves a large urban and rural area, much of which has suffered very high unemployment levels for many years. It is well provided with continuing education institutions, including a university and polytechnic which has developed a reputation for its sympathetic response to the needs of mature students.

The genesis of Service C was in 1976-77, when two groups with an interest in adult education were meeting in the city and arriving at similar conclusions about the need for a Service to advise on adult education opportunities, vocational opportunities and grant availability. The first group consisted of representatives from professional bodies concerned with providing adult education who were meeting for a series of seminars. The second was a group of consumers of adult education, ex-students from a New Opportunities for Women course run by the Adult Education Department of the university, who tried to form an Advisory Centre for Education and Employment.

The problems in finding premises and funds soon loomed large, and, following a conference in March 1978, the two groups merged when a steering committee was convened under the name of Service C to launch the initiative. The steering committee included representatives from three LEAs (later joined by a fourth) and from major educational or other elected institutions which desired membership, plus some co-opted members. It still survives as the management committee, in whom all powers of finance, operation and policy are vested. Thus it represents the collaborative nature of the venture and its independence in constitution from the interested parent bodies.

The aims and operation of Service C have been described in the Report to its second Annual Conference in 1980:

...From its inception the Steering Committee was convinced that a 'low cost' model would be most appropriate... It was also regarded as important to call upon those already committed to providing advice themselves. The whole concept of provision of an adult education advisory service depends on the interaction of the various agencies involved and a collaborative activity therefore seems appropriate. It was from this standpoint that the idea of a net of link advisers was born; each adviser being open to personal approaches and, where necessary, passing enquiries direct to another adviser in the chain, who may be better able to help. Such contacts are passed direct from adviser to adviser and so do not lose the enquirer before contact has been made. The network of advisers was envisaged to be wider than purely educational contacts as queries would also be including career guidance agencies, voluntary organisations and social agencies.

In order to provide any reasonable service it was thought necessary to identify at least 3 types of enquiry.

1. Straightforward requests for information
2. Enquiries which require counselling help to define their real need
3. Enquiries which call for educational provision not presently available.

In order to deal effectively with the second and third of these categories, volunteer staff will need, over a period of time, a form of training which the organisation should seek to provide...

The networked advisers would, in the main, work within their own organisations. However, it was felt important that a central point be established, both for receiving enquiries and cataloguing appropriate information... The centre should be manned with a view to

a) collecting and disseminating information required by Service C
b) answering queries which come in
c) providing, within the Service C organisation, counselling for those who need help of this kind
d) referring out queries or counselling problems which lie in other fields of expertise (e.g. careers guidance)

The advisers should be kept in touch with each other by means of the directory which lists all those who are willing to act within the network and also details the activities of the centre.

The original concept of the Service was clearly of an independent client-centred facility, not least because, as one member of the steering committee put it:

...If you merely fill courses and merely rely on very crude recruitment and enrolment practices then you will find a lot of square pegs in round holes and you will find higher drop-out. I think I am even more convinced that the further this process goes forward, the more involvement there is of trying to find and place people as near as possible to their aspirations, the more it is likely that we will reduce the drop-out and make the service more effective.

Resources for the initial phase of Service C's activity were obtained informally, with different institutions giving help to provide premises, the directory, telephones, stationery and so on. The Service's centre was opened in September 1978 and for the first six weeks it was staffed by volunteers drawn from the ex-students' group which co-founded the Service, as well as by the steering committee and advisers. More permanent staffing had to be found, to provide a 9-to-5 facility, five days a week; and even though the initial instinct of the Chairman of the steering committee was that,

> ...We did not want to play around with temporary funding from MSC because we all thought that if we went temporary we would be compromising on what we wanted to do

this was, in fact, what had to be accepted, to maintain the centre element of Service C's link-chain-centre structure. The one full-time post, renewable each year, was awarded in November 1978 through the STEP/CEP schemes, which did not permit the occupant of the post more than one year's tenure. Between November 1978 and March 1981 there were four changes of staff in this job. A half-time liaison post, subject to review each year, was instituted in June 1979 on the award of a grant to Service C from the Inner City Partnership, and that post has continued to be held by the same occupant. This member of staff was one of the earliest interested members of the student group co-founders and was considered to have made a major contribution to the sense of continuity within the Service.*

The question of premises was solved at first when one of the parent institutions offered the use of a room, providing a base for the Service between September 1978 and August 1980, until the building containing it was condemned. Following two months in an empty office, without light or heat, a new room was made available by yet another parent institution, the polytechnic, which Service C has inhabited ever since. Both premises have proved adequate, though by no means ideal. The present site, while closer to the town centre than the earlier one, is nevertheless situated in a thoroughfare not much frequented by the general public. It is a quiet terrace approximately 200 yards from one of the city's busiest shopping areas, but isolated by new motorway routes and frequented mainly by students from the polytechnic and by visitors to an office block, where many community agencies reside. Service C occupies a single first-floor room in one house on the terrace. It is not advertised externally, though a banner on the mezzanine between ground and first floors indicates its presence once the client has entered the house. A client would have to be seeking it out rather than 'happening' upon it. The room itself harbours material

---

*In June 1981 a third appointment was obtained via a neighbouring CEP Agency for a full-time outreach worker in a specific locality, and that post is also renewable after a year.

belonging to the parent institution and offers limited storage space and few materials for making staff and clientele relaxed and comfortable. Like Services A and B, Service C has no private copying or printing facilities and, for a Service which relies so heavily upon telephone contact, a restrictive single telephone line. For clients who do visit, there is no waiting room, and in a busy period one customer could be waiting in the same room where another's consultation is taking place. Some attempt at privacy has been attempted by the recent introduction of a screen.

A member of the steering committee recalls that the centre was to play, 'a key but humble part' i.e. 'to facilitate sensible referral, to stimulate concern for the adult student and to encourage agencies and authorities to move beyond the crudity of mere publicity towards student-centred advice and information'. Assessment of the first of these objectives may be gauged from the number of enquiries dealt with centrally (the Service has always experienced difficulty in recording bilateral enquiries, i.e. adviser to adviser, which use the directory but do not go through the centre). From September 1978 to May 1979, 301 contacts were handled; from June 1979 to March 1980, the figure was 415; and from April 1980 to March 1981, 1026. The last figure does not include approximately 1000 enquiries handled via an EGSA-manned central library stand during the September enrolment period — when the resources of the Service have always been stretched to the limits and proper recording of numbers has been impossible. Our research was carried out during the ninth month of the fourth year of operation, and client contacts had already reached 1640, rising to 2125 by the end of the year, March 1982. This figure again excludes an estimated 1300 enquiries handled at the library stand and at a similar venture held in a nearby shopping-centre.

Service C's attention to liaison and outreach was said to have extended the awareness of the public and of the relevant institutions to the existence and functions of the Service; the development of information displays and the free telephone extension in City C's central library (linking the library enquirer directly to the EGSA) made the Service more accessible and more widely known. More recently, the Service has begun to research and produce information sheets *(Fees and the unemployed, Childcare facilities in Further Education* and *Facilities for Disabled People in Further Education* were published in 1981-82) and has published two occasional papers on key issues in continuing education. Use of the public media has been limited due to cost, though the Service enjoyed some time allocation on local radio in August 1980 and information about its services was included in a six-page supplement (on continuing education) circulated via a local free newspaper to the majority of homes in the city in summer 1981. Responding to the ACACE report, *Links to learning,* Service C commented:

...It is more costly and labour intensive to get information to people who are not normal users of services such as the library than to those who use the services and who, therefore, are relatively easy to reach through well tried and tested methods.

In all, Service C, at the time of our research, was understood to operate as a central information, basic advice and assisted referral point, which linked clients to a network of advisers in a wide variety of institutions. Information as the prime (and most-demanded) function was confirmed by reference to the Service's annual report. During the period 1981-82, the Service assessed the perceived nature of its enquiries thus: 76% information, 19% advice, 5% guidance. These classifications were defined as follows:

'Information'   —the enquirer has not needed to give personal information

'Advice'   —the enquirer has given some personal information but no 'transactions' need to have taken place

'Guidance'   —the enquirer gave personal information and it is suspected that some interaction needs to take place with the adviser.

These classifications offer some insight into why it is apparently possible for an information-oriented Service to deal with a vastly greater number of clients than those which emphasise counselling. Service C also operated primarily by telephone; in 1981-82, no fewer than 73% of its contacts were handled in this way. It should be noted that Service C's relationship with its central library was a particularly fruitful one, and in stark contrast with Service B and its library. The City C central library had willingly given over the bulk of its local continuing education enquiries to the EGSA, including those made at the peak enrolment times. From the library's viewpoint, this policy not only relieved their own huge burden of enquiries, but also provided a better service to the client. The unmanned permanent Service C display in the central library to which all relevant enquiries were normally immediately directed was supplemented in 1981 by a free telephone link providing direct contact with the Service. In its first year of operation, this telephone facility alone provided the Service with 18% of its total contacts.*

In considering the operation of Service C, our attention was drawn to a number of fundamental issues which are considered below.

A. Even though a 'low-budget' model was adopted from its inception, to ensure survival, Service C has always felt the insecurity of its funding very keenly. As examples, its 1981 report noted that:

...There are real worries about how long the service can manage to continue on such an uncertain basis. At almost any other time in recent

---

*Service C's relationship with its public library service is considered in detail in the Project's Report to the British Library.

history our activities would have been recognised for mainstream funding.

and in 1982:

...Our funding is temporary and all our efforts to obtain a more secure financial base have failed... There appears to be no mechanism today by which a successful organisation which is meeting a clearly articulated need, can obtain permanent funding.

Negotiations with the Regional Advisory Council for Further Education and with individual LEAs were alike abortive and have forced the Service to depend on MSC, Inner City Partnership and 'hidden' funding or donations. Of these, MSC funding for the Service's one full-time post has been the most problematic, both for its temporariness and for the conditions imposed. The history of the tenure of this post is:

Occupant	Period of tenure	Conditions Applied
1	Nov 1978 – Nov 1979	Preference to be given to disabled person
2	Nov – Dec 1979	Preference to be given to disabled person
Vacant	Jan – Mar 1980	Review of the post by MSC left Service C with a vacancy
3	Mar 1980 – Mar 1981	Preference to disabled still a principal criterion
4	Mar 1981 –	Job only available to disabled person

MSC programme policy changes from 1st April 1981 left Service C with the anxiety that 'There is no guarantee that we can make the post fit into new criteria although it is hoped we can do so'. The half-time Inner City Partnership post also caused concern; it was awarded for a five-year period, but on an annually-renewable basis. It was clear that Service C is unable to appoint or retain such applicants as might be attracted by a permanent situation. The present staff, in fact, all indicated that it was more by accident than by intention that they were led to apply for the EGSA post, and that there was little in their previous experience that might have indicated such a choice. It was felt that if the Service does obtain by this system employees with anything like the requisite and highly exacting range of skills, then it is more a result of good luck than of planned management. There was also a strong feeling amongst the centre's officers that motivation was bound to be weakened in a situation in which one was receiving constant encouragement to look around for a more permanent situation, particularly as one approached the termination of the contract a time at which, in other circumstances, one might be reaching a peak in effectiveness. An additional problem in staffing a Service by this method is that each officer has technically a different employer, with the result that there is little consistency or logic in the system by which their jobs are graded and their salaries established. (Negotiations were going on to improve the situation, but Service C had no autonomy to rectify such matters.)

B. A feature of the Service thus developed was that each job is differentiated from the others, and one officer felt that each individual's sphere of operation was actually becoming more rigidly defined with time. This was a development which the staff unanimously regretted, for those confined to the office felt the need to go out and visit those institutions and advisers to whom they were frequently referring people, while the outreach workers felt the need for more contact with the central office and more opportunities to handle contacts with the public. All staff felt they might be better employed in a more integrated system.

C. There was general agreement amongst the centre's officers that, considering the amount of information to absorb and the range of skills to be developed, the period of time for a new member of staff even to begin to come to terms with the job was at least 'a few months'. A training programme would have facilitated this period of 'settling in'; even though realistic limits would have to be set on that programme when resources are limited and the period of return for investment is short. However, before 1981, training consisted of a fairly random pattern of institutional visits and in-house talks from advisers whenever the latter could offer some of their already stretched services. During 1981 this pattern continued, still somewhat loosely connected, but was supplemented by two innovations. The first involved two linked sessions geared to developing skills in offering clients advice and counselling. This was received with varying degrees of enthusiasm, according to whether the individual centre officer perceived the Service as primarily informational or advisory in its function. The second arose from a decision to institute more systematic monitoring of the work of the centre. A one-hour weekly case-review meeting was introduced, to function as both a monitoring and a training opportunity. This scheme won staff approval, since it provided a regular and reliable link with the advisory system. It was understood that 1982 would bring further innovation and more careful structuring of the training programme, following the report of a sub-committee in the autumn of 1981. This recommended that a basic course be offered at the beginning of each new appointment, to include training in understanding the educational opportunities available to adults, in counselling skills, and in systematic recording of information. It was intended to be supplemented by in-service training, which would integrate staff roles to a greater degree. It was recommended that this programme be completed in the first three months of the new appointment to equip centre officers as well as possible for the pressured summer period.

D. In many ways the linked-adviser system was considered to be one of Service C's strengths, in that it tied together many disparate organisations and promoted a better understanding among them, and that it made available to the Service a wide range of expertise and support. However, there were ambiguities and conflicting understandings which appeared to prevent it from operating efficiently. One officer summarised it thus:

> ...Probably the original concept of (Service C) amongst the professional providers of adult education was that enquiries would come in to the workers, who would then channel them on to the appropriate people. These would be amongst the Advisers in the Linked Advisers Directory, which all Advisers would have so that they could also pass on enquiries made direct to them to the appropriate Adviser. In practice, what was soon happening was that many enquiries *were* made direct to Advisers, who were then passing them on to the (EGSA) office to deal with. In addition, local education authorities were sending people along to us, as were other agencies, so that many enquirers who arrived at Service C had already been elsewhere and had been referred to us.

There were two kinds of response to this development: one may be illustrated by the comment from a steering committee member,

> ...It was supposed to facilitate referral between Advisers and my own view is that we need to go back and replenish the roots — that the Advisers need re-activating, otherwise we are, I think, in danger of making it too reliant on the actual workers...that will not work, because the work will escalate and the Advisers not know precisely what is happening

while the other view is explicit in this account from a centre officer:

> ...We agreed that we shouldn't just pass these enquiries straight on to someone else again, but deal with them ourselves wherever possible...I feel it is heading the wrong way, to just pass the buck, and it makes us seem like just another agency interested in the numbers game and not really interested in the individual.

There was no guarantee that Advisers were always the 'right' people for the task when choice was often dictated by bureaucratic principles rather than relevant skills. The fact that the original order of referral has been regularly inverted suggests that Advisers themselves did not always see themselves as appropriate sources of advice and counselling, or even of information. Additionally, while Service C has enjoyed enthusiastic attendance of many Advisers at its Annual Conferences, training events have not been supported. These matters confirmed one centre officer's view that Advisers:

> ...may know an awful lot about the actual course that they teach in their college at that particular time, but it does not follow at all that they will know anything at all about what other people do.

Officers also acknowledged difficulty in contacting Advisers at times, particularly during the busy summer period when institutions are closed and staff often on holiday, at the very time when Service C is in greatest need of its contacts. Often the most helpful and flexible Advisers were the most difficult to contact because their services were so much in demand. There was no doubt that members of the steering committee and a small range of Advisers beyond it had been accessible and supportive above and beyond the call of duty, but with the EGSA Directory by then listing over eighty Advisers, it would have been unrealistic to expect that all should offer equal service or have equal understanding of the aims of the Service. There were also some gaps in the Adviser system; for example, the main body of City C's university was unrepresented and relationships with more outlying institutions needed improvement.

In all it would appear that Advisers were most frequently used to supplement information and to facilitate a client's pursuit of a specific option rather than to give general advice as had been the original intent. Service C was clearly becoming a more office-centred guidance service. In that case some informants felt that more attention needed to be given to advice and counselling skills, as opposed to information skills, than had hitherto been the case.

E. Both in its original concept and in practice, Service C has recognised a need for advocacy and feedback activities. Advocacy was said to be offered to clients from time to time, and we were given examples of this form of implementation. Feedback was also given on an informal basis, sometimes with very positive results. In all, however, Service C saw this as an area demanding development:

> ...Are we going to be a pressure group and try and put forward people's viewpoints? I mean, present cases to Education Authorities and say, 'Look, you are stopping so many people training to do this, that and the other'... I think if education is generally sort of being squeezed and there are so many unemployed people who obviously need it more, I think we are going to have to look at our role, at what we are doing, whether we are just passing on information about what there is or whether we are going to try and be a sort of intermediary between the two... We have only done very small things in that field in the past...

Both advocacy and feedback are, of course, linked with client follow-up. As with the other Services participating in the research, there was currently no formal provision for the follow-up of clients, to determine how successful they had been in pursuing their enquiries or how satisfied they were with the assistance received. Clients were invited to contact the Service again if they were unsuccessful, and in some cases they responded with thanks when an enquiry had led to success.

Advisers saw a strength in the very survival of Service C against all the odds in a crippling economic climate which, as one put it, 'has hit educational opportunities for adults worse than it hit any other section'. Given all the restrictions and problems in running a low budget Service, there was a shared pleasure in just how much had been achieved, and a modest confidence that, 'We have helped rather than hindered on balance a fairly substantial number of people'.

It was also considered a strong point that Service C, while it was offered good support from many institutions, remained independent of them all, since it was felt that only by such means could it be seen to offer truly impartial advice and be able to attract clients who were not yet ready to approach specific educational institutions.

It was also able to function not just as a central link for the public, but as a central link between institutions too. As one centre worker put it,

> ...It's been successful in bringing the advisers together. A lot of them were personal and business contacts beforehand, but with such things as the general meeting, annual meeting, or maybe using the Directory if they have an inappropriate enquiry...put them in touch with someone else, I think it's made them more aware of what other people are offering. It's also made them more aware of the need for an educational advisory service, and they could also, I suppose, be aware of the fact that if it wasn't for this Service they would lose a lot of their customers.

On the other hand, the problems that this Service experienced with funding were reiterated as the major obstacle to development and expansion. It was widely acknowledged by centre officers and advisers that to run even the current system efficiently would require a number of additional personnel, without beginning to consider expansion of the Service into areas which clamoured for attention. As one of the centre's staff observed:

> ...I have always been particularly worried that we raise expectations and put up a lot of publicity and then cannot cope with the result. I am rather cautious and I tend to think that you should have the manpower first, and then you can raise expectations and put out more publicity and it does not matter if you are flooded with enquiries, because you can cope.

There was an argument for resisting such development of an essentially low-budget facility on the grounds that the lower the overall cost, the more realistic might be its claim for mainstream funding. It was considered regrettable that in the meantime Service C must blinker its vision and suffer the everyday frustrations of working with unrealistic demands on its time for the sake of a hope which, in the short-term at least, was to be viewed as bleak. The incentive for development was doubly weakened by the lack of any certainty about being able to continue even at the present rate beyond a finite period of time.

Service D

Service D is located in a traditionally working-class inner-London borough, which now has a large multiracial population. Its population is understood to have the second lowest level of formal academic attainments in the London area. At the same time, the borough has a wide range of formal and informal continuing education providers, at all levels from a very active literacy provision to a large polytechnic.

The initial impetus for the setting up of Service D derived from the experiences of local adult literacy workers, other educationists and community groups, whose work had led them to recognise the urgent need for such a service. It was the local Literacy Organiser who called a meeting of interested parties in March 1978, from which was formed a working party and which marked the inception of the Service — the first in Inner London. (The same Literacy Organiser serves Service D today as its Management Committee Convenor). Some funds from the borough (£300), and postal, printing, and office facilities from various local educational establishments permitted a short initial phase of research and investigation, leading to the opening of the Service to the public in September 1978. It was the working party's view that growth should be 'within the framework of a phased development programme, ultimately establishing an education shop on the high street'. In an unpublished paper on the development of the project, it was noted:

...To simply throw open our doors from the start would have been irresponsible, as the quality of the Service would have suffered.

The new Service needed to achieve an intimate knowledge of its locality and the social conditions prevailing there and to have enough time and accumulated experience to treat enquiries, where appropriate, as more than informational ones. At the same time it was considered essential that the Service should be independently located rather than attached to any particular institution.

So Service D opened to the public in a small office in the 'neutral' premises of the local Citizens' Advice Bureau for seven and a half hours per week. These premises were considered far from ideal, but they did provide a base for the Service's operations for the following two years. In November 1980 the Service moved into its own shop-front premises in a busy high-street location, from where it has operated, largely on a drop-in basis, ever since.

The function orientation of Service D may be gathered from a statement of the Service's objectives written by its Convenor in 1980:

...a) The objects for which the Service is incorporated are to provide, maintain, improve and advance education particularly by:

Providing (without charge) an education guidance and counselling service to all adults, but primarily those living or working whether in education establishments or not or studying in the Borough.

Providing information services on education opportunities for adults in the vocational, non-vocational and recreational fields.

Financing research in the educational provision and educational guidance provision available within and serving the Borough as to suitability of existing courses in all respects and to ascertain unmet needs.

Promoting the satisfaction of any identified educational need of the residents of the Borough.

b) Education information alone is insufficient. Active advice is also required to facilitate understanding of the information provided, to relate it to needs, to assess suitability of particular courses. Educational counselling, while more time consuming, is often more cost

61

effective in the long run — it provides the forum in which an enquirer can reach his/her own decisions fully understanding the financial, social and personal implications of his/her choice and often become a highly motivated and successful student.

However, adults may need help not only in making choices (based on information of the whole range of resources) but also in their implementation. This help may take a number of forms: *support* in working through systems of entry procedures, stresses of interview or examination, etc; *advocacy* — negotiation on behalf of the enquirer regarding such issues and entry requirements, timing of courses, grants appeals, ancilliary services etc.

This close contact with individuals and groups in the community allows for the feedback of information on clients' needs into the education system so that the system can take account and respond to them.

The particular emphasis given to feedback by this Service is underlined in its First Annual Report:

...We have also been successful in filling certain gaps in local educational provision and are in constant dialogue with a variety of agencies on this most urgent topic. It is the fitting of education and training provision to the needs of local people and not simply fitting people to what currently exists which is the crux of the matter.

Financial independence from educational providers as a means of assuring the Service's prime loyalty to its clients' needs is very apparent with this Service, since, in the view of one of its workers, 'purse strings and policy strings can be pulled together'. Its funding over the last four years has been an innovative and precarious mix, from public and charitable sources, as follows:

Sept 1978:   Service set up on interim pooled resources.

Nov/Dec 1978:   £3,800 attracted to the Service from three charitable sources.

July/Dec 1979:   The same three sources gave a further £4,700 and a fourth charity £100.

July 1979:   LEA funds were provided to meet the salary of the full-time worker, ten hours secretarial assistance and £750 expenses, as recurrent funds subject to satisfactory development.

Sept 1980:   The Service became a company limited by guarantee and gained charitable status, to cover the possibility of attracting further funds.

Dec 1980:   £1,300 from three charitable sources (one donation of £1,000 is on-going for three years).

1981-82:   Corporate membership subscriptions were invited from educational institutions. Six subscribed, raising additional income of £450.

March 1982:   £8,000 was received from two charitable sources, to assist in meeting the cost of another full-time worker.

The Service has also enjoyed throughout its existence small amounts of 'hidden' funding and donations in kind from a variety of sympathetic institutions.

At the time of research, Service D was well-established in its shop-front premises. Its staff consisted of the project co-ordinator, first appointed in 1979, and a second full-time worker (who had formerly worked for Service D on a part-time basis), working as a counsellor with a substantial outreach brief. The Service also had a part-time secretary/receptionist, working for twenty hours a week. The shop itself is quite small and lacks privacy, but is brightly decorated, and simply but adequately furnished. The reception/browsing area houses display racks offering local brochures and information leaflets, some chairs and the secretary's desk and telephone, and filing cabinets. The shop window is used to display information on relevant facilities and courses. The design of the shop conveys a 'drop in' image which encourages clients to use it in much the same way as any other high-street shop. It is possible for clients visiting Service D to use the browsing facilities without contact with its workers, though our observations indicated that clients normally sought, or were offered, attention from one of the staff. The secretary was able to provide assistance with the brochures, but in most cases directed the client to whichever of the full-time workers was available. Pre-arranged appointments were common, but most often the client was interviewed spontaneously. These interviews took as long as was necessary, i.e. there was no pre-set time limit. However, the Service perceived it as important not to overload the client with information, but to encourage return visits when further assistance was required. The shop was open from 10am to 5pm on Tuesdays and Thursdays, from 10am to 8pm on Wednesdays, and from 10am to 1pm on Fridays and Saturdays. It closed on Sundays and Mondays.

This 'drop-in' shop-front concept was thought to be vindicated by an analysis of the first year's enquiries at the new premises. A total of just over 1,000 clients used the shop during the period November 1980 — November 1981, of whom over a quarter sought further contact with the Service. These numbers were considered to compare very favourably with the Service's first location, where approximately 1,000 clients were seen in the two years of operation. The Service's Annual Report (1982) identified the following groups of users during the Service's first year in its shop:

(a) 80% were borough residents.
(b) 55% were women.
(c) 30% were from minority ethnic groups.

63

(d) 40% were unemployed (with a significant number of those in employment seeking to upgrade their skills to keep ahead of unemployment).

The new location, in comparison with the CAB premises, attracted a larger proportion of very local clients, while the women, ethnic minority and unemployed groups remained roughly the same. The Service gauged itself to be involved in offering counselling to around half of its clients. This activity, together with its implementation work, was very time-intensive. On its present level of staffing, with clients averaging twenty per week over the year, the Service was considered to be working at full stretch.

Our discussions with key informants at Service D focussed on a number of important developmental issues, which are considered below.

A. Despite the Service's bold initiatives in funding, it has long sought mainstream funding which will offer a secure base for development, while at the same time permitting full independence of operation. Present funding arrangements are much more stable than in the Service's early days. In December 1980, for example, a member of the staff commented that:

> ...the major preoccupation of the last three months has been getting the money to keep this thing alive so that we can then go out and say to people, 'This is what we do'. We don't want to go out and say to people, 'This is what we were doing but we've run out of money...'

But relative security has been obtained only through protracted negotiations, often inordinately time-consuming, which have taken staff away from actually operating the Service. Until March 1982, the Service's Co-ordinator was also the only full-time member of staff, whose duties, apart from fund-raising and advice and counselling, included administration, staff training, report-writing, management committee duties, researching for and following-up enquiries, logging feedback from clients and lobbying providers. The Service has, however, maintained a strong objection in principle to the use of MSC-funded personnel and has a guarded response to the use of volunteers. Volunteers were used in the first phase of the Service's development (for example, they helped to compile the Service's card index of local courses), but their potential as generalist advisers in the Service was not regarded positively. As one Service worker commented:

> ...Personally, I'm against the use of volunteers... I think the work we are trying to do is far too important not to be funded properly and realistically...(from my previous experience) the actual task of co-ordinating what (the volunteers) were doing was taking away the person who was meant to be co-ordinating the project as a whole, and it was also difficult to monitor what was going on in the interaction between the volunteers and the users of the Service.

Were the Service in a position where it was forced to use volunteers, a very careful training would be considered essential.

B. It is clear that the Service's workers showed a strong sense of responsibility for the consequences for their clients of their referrals or recommendations.

Between one quarter and one third of clients were understood to have visited the Service more than once in pursuit of their enquiry. This policy of actively encouraging sustained contact ensured a steady (though small) feed-back on clients' perceptions of the attitudes of educational providers and the quality of their courses. The Service also saw itself as having an important role for adults already enrolled in courses:

> ...We've already seen people coming in who have been in educational institutions...where they haven't had a good time and they've had nobody to talk to because they can't talk to the people who are tutoring them...people come in and say, 'That course is lousy for me. What else can I do?' and we can pass them on to somewhere else...

Such information, both positive and negative, was highly valued by the workers in guiding other clients and was also conveyed informally to appropriate professional contacts, though at all times with tact and diplomacy. At the same time, the Service acknowledged that its role in feedback was under-developed because of imperfect record-keeping and resources too stretched to permit the systematic follow-up of its clients. Major policy-makers responded, 'It's no good talking in hypothetical terms and giving us anecdotal evidence — we want hard facts'. Nevertheless, Service D had achieved some notable successes in its negotiations with institutions for changes in provision.

C. Service workers also expressed considerable concern about their links with educational providers in the locality.

While well-provided with sympathetic contacts (indeed, the Service maintained a card index of those who had proved useful), the difficulties in 'trying to spread ourselves over six or eight colleges, three institutes and three of four polys at once' were keenly felt. Service workers themselves had become 'professional enquirers', with ample first-hand experience of the difficulties of getting through to 'the right person'. Two strategies were under consideration to improve matters. The first was to recruit a team of cross-institution subject specialists, to whom referrals could be made on a subject-specific rather than institution-specific basis. Such specialists might also be encouraged to give sessions at the shop; and in this respect the Service saw a useful role for volunteers. The second strategy was to develop a model for intra-institution networking which might be tested at a local college and later applied to others. In the meantime, Service D maintained a watchful eye on untried contacts and had also (though exceptionally) changed its contact person in an institution, when considered necessary. Development of institutional and agency outreach, as well as to new client groups, was seen as an urgent priority and one which might now be pursued with the full-time appointment of an outreach worker.

Service D manifests perhaps the strongest commitment to client-centred educational guidance of all the four Services taking part in our research, and the most clearly articulated identification with disadvantaged groups. It is also a pioneer Service, the first of this particular kind in the UK, and has done much to encourage other Services in the London area as well as to promote the development of EGSAs nationally. It appeared to us that Service D has a very clear view of its philosophy and role; but insecurities of funding have perforce distracted energy from areas of operational growth and development. In this respect, Service D represents an interesting contrast with the advantages of 'low-resource' models such as Service A.

Overview

We noted in Chapter 2 that 'the linked values of improved access, collaborative provision, independence, client-centredness and advocacy are cumulatively what marks out a new ethos of educational guidance'; and, although sometimes interpreted in different ways, they are values clearly exhibited by the EGSAs taking part in our research. All four have arisen from a firm conviction that adults are in need of a whole range of preliminary assistance if continuing education is to be genuinely open to them. They have been initiated, and continue to be supported, in a genuinely collaborative way. Collaboration has also strengthened independence, which itself is manifested in the 'neutral' premises chosen as these Services' operational bases. All are clearly concerned to maintain a client-centred approach, rather than acting as a collective recruitment agency, and have at least begun to consider — or have actually embarked upon — an advocacy role. At the same time, there are important differences in attitudes and operational approach, which are not only attributable to vagaries of funding. It seems to us that these differences raise some fundamental issues of practice.

All Services stressed the importance of moving beyond 'simple' information provision, yet in the 'numbers game' it is these enquiries, seen as relatively non-time-consuming, which boost annual client contact totals. It is not appropriate to disregard numbers of contacts, since it is axiomatic that an 'access' agency is of little worth if nobody uses it. Our Services, however, were under pressure to demonstrate extent of demand and not only from sponsors; growth in numbers of client contacts reinforced the Service's own motivation and also maintained credibility with providers. The acceptance of no-growth or at least low-growth, in the interests of clients, is not always an acceptable option.

It is our view that the need which EGSAs meet may be demonstrated not only in the numbers of clients served, but also in what is done on their behalf. Our Services perceived themselves to attend closely to the needs of their clients during interview, but, with the exception of Service D, were little able to follow them through. The systematic follow-up of clients, while time-consuming, appears to be a matter of considerable importance, not only for the client but also for the Service, with implications for its self-monitoring and the feed-back role. A thorough approach to record-keeping is implicit here.

In theory, follow-up may be little necessary in a system where EGSA and links/advisers/networks are in sympathy. Our evidence suggests that, however termed, such contacts in educational institutions and in other relevant agencies need to be carefully selected, trained and given on-going support, to provide adequately the assistance asked from them. Such assistance cannot be automatically assumed. This carries implications for the importance of outreach and for reconsideration of the role of the Service's central staff.

Our four Services demonstrated clear differences of opinion on the question of staffing, which raised matters of principle as well as funding. From an operational viewpoint, evidence suggests that centre staff continuity is an important matter, but training is a vital one, given the complexity of the guidance process in each of the functions considered in Chapter 3. This underlines the importance of a substantial 'breaking-in' period for new Services and also for each new member of staff.

The ingenuity, determination and commitment displayed by the four Services taking part in our research, in the face of often implacable indifference from the appropriate funding bodies, is remarkable. Each has achieved a solution which brings advantages as well as disadvantages; for example, an 'un-cuttable' Service may also be a 'low-profile' Service. The availability — or otherwise — of funding crucially affects the structure and operation of Services. Together with the Service's guiding ethos, it may profoundly affect the nature of the assistance provided to clients and the Service's view of what clients should, or are able, to do for themselves.

CHAPTER 6
THE CLIENTS

Introduction

The purpose of this chapter is to present some background data about the seventy-six people who constituted our case-load from the four EGSAs and to examine some features of the personal contexts in which the enquiries were made. We also consider how the clients came to make contact with the EGSA and what they were enquiring about. The last section reviews the implications of our findings.

We cannot say definitely whether the clients we recruited were fully representative of the four EGSAs' users, since sometimes the Service's own records did not permit of appropriate comparison. Where comparative data were available, they have been extrapolated and are referred to in the text, as are factors specific to each Service which may have affected the profile of the sample.

Characteristics of the sample

Analyses of clients by age, marital status, number and age of dependent children, occupation, spouses' occupation, school leaving age, type of school attended, highest educational qualifications on leaving school and post-school, and other learning experiences undertaken since leaving school are given in Tables 1 to 14. In broad terms, these educational guidance clients presented the following characteristics:

Table 1: Client sample: age

Age group (years)	Number of clients (n=76)	Total %
Under 20	5	7
20 — 24	22	29
25 — 29	19	25
30 — 34	10	13
35 — 39	12	16
40 — 44	1	1
45 — 49	2	3
50 — 54	2	3
55 — 59	2	3
60 — 64	1	1
65+	0	0

Table 2: Client sample: marital status

	Married (n=35)	%	Single (n=41)	%	Total (n=76)	%
Male	13	37	21	51	34	45
Female	22	63	20	49	42	55

Table 3: Client sample: dependent children

Number of children	Number of clients (n=76)	Total %
None	47	62
One	10	13
Two	12	16
Three	5	7
Four or more	2	3

Table 4: Client sample: age of youngest dependent child

Age group (years)	Number of children (n=29)	Total %
0 — 4	5	17
5 — 8	10	34
9 — 16	9	31
16+ in full-time education	2	7
No information	3	10

Table 5: Client sample: occupation

Occupational group	Number of clients (n=76)	Total %
Housewife	12	16
Admin and managerial	3	4
Teacher/lecturer	1	1
Other professional	2	3
Part-qualified junior professional	3	4
Technical and engineering	4	5
Clerical and office	6	8
Sales and service — skilled	2	3
Sales and service — unskilled	5	7
Labourers	1	1
Unemployed	33	43
Students	2	3
Retired	0	0
Other	2	3

Table 6: Client sample: occupation or previous occupation if unemployed or housewife

Occupational group	Number of clients (n=76)	Total %
Admin and managerial	4	5
Teachers/lecturers	4	5
Other professional	5	7
Part-qualified junior professional	7	9
Technical and engineering	12	16
Clerical and office	23	30
Sales and service — skilled	5	7
Sales and service — unskilled	7	9
Labourers	2	3
Students	3	4
Retired	0	0
Other	4	5

1. There were rather more women than men: 55% and 45% respectively (Table 2). This accords with Services C and Ds' annual totals, but not with quarterly records for Service B, where men predominated in the proportion 56% to 44%. In our sample, Service C attracted the highest proportion of women (75%).

2. Approximately nine out of ten clients were age thirty-nine years or less (Table 1). This compares with seven out of ten in Service B's analysis and with Service D's statement that '80% of all users are over twenty-one years of age, with a significant majority in the twenty-one to thirty-five age group'. Service D appeared to attract rather younger clients than the other Services taking part in the research.

3. There were slightly more single than married people in the sample: 54% and 46% respectively (Table 2). At Service D, however, thirteen (81%) of the sample were single. Women predominated in the 'married' group in the ratio 2:1.

4. Almost two-thirds of clients had no dependent children (Table 3). For those clients with children, at least two-thirds had a child of compulsory school age. (Table 4).

5. Nearly six out of ten (59%) clients were not in employment at the time of the research (full-time students excluded). This group comprised twelve (16%) women who categorised themselves as housewives, but who in almost all cases were looking for work; and thirty-three (43%) unemployed persons (Table 5). This last figure accords approximately with the Services' own totals; Service B recorded 50% of its clients as unemployed and Service D 40%.

Table 7: Client sample: spouses' occupations

Occupation group	Number of spouses (n=35)	Total %
Housewife	3	9
Admin and managerial	3	9
Teachers/lecturers	2	6
Other professional	1	3
Part-qualified junior professional	0	0
Technical and engineering	8	23
Clerical and office	5	14
Sales and service — skilled	7	20
Sales and service — unskilled	1	3
Labourers	1	3
Unemployed	2	6
Students	0	0
Retired	0	0
Other	1	3
No information	1	3

Table 8: Client sample: age on leaving school

Age group (years)	Number of clients (n=76)	Total %
Under 16	26	34
16 — 18	50	66

6. Excluding the 'housewife' and 'unemployed' groups, Table 5 shows a slight predominance of the middle-range employment categories: i.e. technical and engineering; clerical and office; and skilled sales and service. Table 6 shows that, when the previous occupations of housewives and unemployed persons are taken into account, these categories greatly predominate, accounting for over half (53%) of clients' employment. Only nine (12%) clients fell into the 'unskilled' grouping. Service D attracted the highest number of these clients (five), while Service C had none. The same pattern is apparent in spouses' employment (Table 7).

7. Not surprisingly, in view of the relative youthfulness of the sample, only about one in three of the sample left school at age fifteen years or below (Table 8). (NB. The school-leaving age was raised from fifteen to sixteen years in 1972). Service B attracted the highest proportion of early school-levers (60%); it also attracted the highest proportion of clients aged thirty years and over (65%).

8. Type of school attended, as shown in Table 9, was fairly evenly spread between grammar/high, comprehensive and secondary modern, though there were wide variations between individual Services' samples. Thus, Service C had the highest proportion of grammar/high school attenders (45%) and Service D the lowest (12.5%); Service A the highest proportion of comprehensive school attenders (50%), Service B the lowest (15%); Service B the highest proportion of secondary modern school attenders (55%) and Service D the lowest (19%).

Table 9: Client sample: type of school attended

School	Number of clients (n=76)	Total %
Grammar/high	21	28
Comprehensive	26	34
Secondary modern	22	29
Public	0	0
Other	5	7
No information	2	3

Table 10: Client sample: highest educational qualifications on leaving school

Type of qualification	Number of clients (n=76)	Total %
None	32	42
CSE/RSA 1+ subjects	6	8
GCE 'O' level/School Certificate 1—4 subjects	15	20
GCE 'O' level/School Certificate 5+ subjects	9	12
GCE 'A' level/Higher Certificate 1 subject	2	3
GCE 'A' level/Higher Certificate 2+ subjects	10	13
Other	2	3

Table 11: Client sample: highest qualifications gained since leaving school

Type of qualification	Number of clients gaining qualification (n=76)	Total %
None	26	32
CSE/RSA 1 or more subjects	9	11
GCE 'O' level/School Certificate 1—4 subjects	3	4
GCE 'O' level/School Certificate 5+ subjects	0	0
GCE 'A' level/Higher Certificate 1 subject	4	5
GCE 'A' level/Higher Certificate 2+ subjects	1	1
ONC/OND	5	6
HNC/HND	5	6
Teaching Certificate	2	2
University Diploma	4	5
First Degree	8	10
Higher Degree	3	4
Other (1)	11	14

[1] Includes vocational qualifications, e.g. SRN, which some clients gained in conjunction with educational qualifications.

Table 12: Client sample: other learning experiences in last five years

| | Formal courses | | Independent learning | |
	Number of clients (n=76)	Total %	Number of clients (n=76)	Total %
Yes	54	71	26	34
No	22	29	50	66

Table 13: Client sample: usage of formal courses

Type of course taken	Number of instances of client usage (n=104)	Total usage of all courses %
*Craft:		
personal care and household economy	4	4
leisure time enjoyment	7	7
†Physical skills:		
maintenance of health and fitness	2	2
leisure time enjoyment	5	5
‡Intellectual and cognitive skills: languages (non-examinable)	5	5
all others	14	13
Vocational and exam directed	67	64

* *Craft.* Personal care and household economy includes such activities as beauty culture, car maintenance, cooking, dressmaking, gardening, soft furnishing.
Leisure time enjoyment includes such activities as carving and sculpture, drama, drawing, music, photography, pottery.
† *Physical skills.* Maintenance of health and fitness includes keep fit, yoga, etc.
Leisure time enjoyment includes outdoor activities and indoor games, sports and dancing.
‡ *Intellectual and cognitive skills.* All others include history, music, bridge, current affairs, discussion.

Table 14: Client sample: instances of independent learning (see notes to Table 13).

Type of learning undertaken	Number of instances in sample (n=33)	Total %
Craft:		
personal care and household economy	2	6
leisure time enjoyment	7	21
Physical skills:		
maintenance of health and fitness	0	0
leisure time enjoyment	1	3
Intellectual and cognitive skills:		
languages (non-examinable)	2	6
all others	18	55
Vocational and exam-directed	3	9

9. About four out of ten clients had left school with no qualifications; and a further three out of ten with four 'O' levels or less (Table 10). Service C attracted both the lowest proportion of 'no school qualifications' clients (25%) and the highest of 'two "A" levels or more' clients (30%). Service B's clients presented the strongest contrast; proportions for these two groups were 60% and 5% respectively.

10. About one in three clients had not gone on to gain educational qualifications after school and a further 15% had achieved four 'O' levels or less (Table 11). Again, there were major differences between individual Services' samples. 56% of Service D's clients fell into the 'no qualifications post school' category, as opposed to none in the sample drawn from Service C. Service C also attracted the largest proportion of clients having experienced degree-level education; e.g. six of its clients had first degrees.

11. Nearly three-quarters of the sample had engaged in other formal learning experiences over the past five years; and about one-third recognised themselves as having pursued some form of independent learning during the same period (Table 12). The fifty-four clients who had pursued (though not necessarily completed) formal courses had directed their attention primarily to vocational and examination-directed courses (Table 13). Service C clients were again most active here. The twenty-six clients pursuing independent learning were most likely to do so in the intellectual and cognitive skills area (Table 14). Differences in levels of independent learning between Service samples were small.

Motivation

We found that by far the most frequently recurring motivation among this sample was a vocational one, perhaps unsurprisingly in view of the high proportion of unemployed and housewife clients. As D3 (client number 3 in service D), who was unemployed, put it:

> ...Basically to get a job...it's a start, isn't it?...English and Maths, even in manual jobs, it always helps.

However, those in employment were in many cases anxious about redundancy or expressed great dissatisfaction with their current employment. At Service C, for example:

45% were unemployed and urgently seeking new opportunities/ vocational training;

10% were making provision in the face of imminent redundancy;

15% were seeking radical changes in career direction;

15% were seeking to develop skills for the occupation held;

5% actually obtained a job by getting on to an appropriate course quickly; and only

10% had no vocational interest whatsoever in the enquiry presented.

That such a pattern is not untypical of our Services' clients is confirmed in Service C's Report for 1981-82:

> ...An increasing number of our enquirers are from the unemployed whose queries tend to be complex ones which can often not only involve education but fees, regulations, welfare benefits and vocational outcomes.

and in an unpublished paper from Service D, which comments:

> ...a substantial number of those who are in employment could be classified as seeking an upgrading of skills. It has also become noticeable recently that an increasing number of people under threat or notice of redundancy are using the Service.

Two examples from Service B illustrate clearly the backgrounds, motivations and aspirations of such clients. B15 was aged thirty-six, married with three children aged fifteen, fourteen and twelve. She left secondary modern school at fifteen with no educational qualifications. She worked on the shop floor at an engineering firm and was promoted to office work before she was made redundant. Her husband worked at the same firm as a gearcutter and was on short time. She was not a member of the public library, since she preferred knitting to reading because 'there was something to show at the end of it'. She had been to keep fit class once. When she was made redundant she went to the Job Centre and to the Careers Service; she failed the English test for a TOPS course. She came to Service B looking for training for a job. Client B9 was twenty-one years old. He left a comprehensive school (with four 'O' levels and three CSEs), against his parents' wishes, to work at a printing firm. He had been promised day release for further study but found himself employed as 'a machine-minder' with no day-release, so he left and went to the local tax office. He left the tax office to go to an engineering firm, because he was 'promised all sorts', but he ended up as a warehouse labourer. Again he left and after eight months' unemployment he went to a supermarket as a shop assistant. He commented:

> ...You know, at school I worked hard and learnt all these things, got some 'O' levels and some CSEs and I'm stuck here like an idiot, like a parrot on somebody's shoulder just doing their bidding all the time.

This client had done a course in photo-copying at his first job before his day-release was stopped; he also painted at home, with the help of his father. He had not looked for help anywhere else and had come to Service B for advice on how to 'get out of the rut' he was in.

It is evident that vocational motivations and aspirations are also clearly linked with clients' needs for personal fulfilment. Their decision to seek assistance from an EGSA may well coincide with other major issues in their lives, e.g. a realisation that for a multiplicity of reasons they made mistaken early choices, the consequences of which are now no longer tolerable, or a more recent personal crisis. Three clients from Service C further illustrate these points:

> ...I couldn't, under any circumstances, see myself doing the job I'm doing now until I retire...When I went to school, I had to do mock 'O' levels, that sort of thing. I passed those, but when it came to the exams, my family were pushed for cash, and then I went into an apprenticeship as a fitter. (C18)

> ...School? I don't know, the last year, I just couldn't be bothered to go. I felt as if they couldn't teach us any more than I already knew, sort of thing, so I thought what's the point?... I think I was very stupid, because I could have stuck at it and got a few exam results, you know...I split up from my husband about seven months ago, and then I just suddenly realised, 'God, what have you got?' You know what I mean? So I thought I would try and make some sort of life for myself. (C15)

> ...I went for an office job, and Mum and Dad said, 'If you're going for a job like that it'll settle you down'. But I never liked office work at school but the Careers Officer at school was always saying, you know, 'Oh, take office work. You're good at that'...When I said it (art and design) at the careers interview — 'Oh, that's a bad field to go into'. Still, I mean, they were only trying to help, I suppose, but they tried to put me off as much as possible and they never really told me about art schools at all. (C4)

Nature of the enquiries

Table 15 shows the broad nature of the enquiries from both clients' and advisers'* perceptions. It again illustrates the importance to clients of the link between education and employment, with twenty-eight (37%) clients seeking specific career and employment advice and twenty-nine (38%) information on vocational courses. Only eight

---

* The term 'advisers' is used from this point in the text to refer to the guidance workers dealing with the clients, however termed in their specific Service.

77

Table 15: Enquiries: types

	Adviser		Client	
Nature of enquiry*	Number of clients (n=76)	Total %	Number of clients (n=76)	Total %
Leisure and recreational	10	13	8	11
Vocational	30	39	29	38
Academic	19	25	29	38
Career and job	24	32	28	37
Other	9	12	3	4

* Clients and advisers sometimes answered in terms of more than one option.

(11%) clients, seven of whom were from Service C, sought information on non-vocational leisure-type courses, and most of these saw an employment link to their enquiry. (We are not in a position to say whether this was the case with the large number of 'leisure' enquiries which are treated mainly on an information-only basis at peak enrolment times). Again, there were large differences between Services. For example, fifteen (75%) clients at Service B presented career and job enquiries, a figure possibly enhanced because many of its sample were attracted to the Service by a local radio broadcast which emphasised the link between education and employment marketability. In contrast, only one such client was recorded in Service C's sample, perhaps because all such clients were referred to the local Careers Advisory Service. Table 15 also shows important discrepancies between advisers' and clients' perceptions of the broad nature of the enquiry. Only at Service C was there nearly complete unanimity of views and this may be accounted for by the proscribing effect of the use of the telephone, both on clients' presentation and advisers' responses. Discrepancies are most apparent in the 'academic' category, where some advisers seemed to over-interpret the clients' immediate training or employment needs, while there were some occasions when these were not considered at all. A more general explanation of these discrepancies lies in the difficulties that clients had in presenting their real or all their intentions to the adviser. Advisers were not always able to pick up the cues being given and sometimes seemed keen to 'slot in' the client to a particular form of provision.

Table 16: Enquiries: sources through which EGSA discovered

Source	Number of clients (n=76)	Total %
Library	17	22
Local radio	14	18
Educational institution	12	16
Accidental discovery of office	12	16
Job Centre	7	9
Local newspaper	4	5
Telephone directory	4	5
Careers Advisory Service	3	4
Friend	1	1
Other	1	1
No information	1	1

Table 17: Enquiries: proportion of clients seeking help from other sources before approaching the EGSA

Other help sought	Number of clients (n=76)	Total %
Yes	35	46
No	41	54

Table 18: Enquiries: proportion of enquiries directed to other sources before visiting the EGSA

Source	Number of approaches made to each source*	Total %
Educational institution	16	28
Job Centre	15	26
Careers Advisory Service	7	12
Friends and other personal contacts	7	12
Library	6	11
Other	6	11
TOTAL	57	100

* Clients may have approached more than one source, or a single source more than once.

79

Contacting the Service

Table 16 shows the source from which the existence of the EGSA was first discovered by clients. The place of local radio in the Table is largely accounted for by an outreach event organised by Service B. Other than this, the most commonly recurring sources were the public library and educational institutions. Accidental discovery of the Service's office was largely accounted for by Service D (nine clients). In view of Services B and Cs' close connections with their central library, the predominance of the library as a source for clients might be expected, but there were some surprises. While Service C attracted nine (45%) of its clients in this way, Service B, which is located within the library, attracted four (20%) and its sample also had the lowest proportion of library members (65%). Over 80% of Service D's sample were public library members, yet none of them had obtained information on the Service from this source. Table 16 also shows that only ten (13%) clients discovered the existence of their EGSA from the Job Centre or Careers Advisory Service. At the same time, Table 17 shows that almost half the clients had sought help from other sources before approaching the EGSA. This figure was highest at Service C (70%) and lowest at Service B (30%). Table 18 shows that approaches to the Job Centre or Careers Advisory Service accounted for over one-third of all such contacts. The library, however, accounts for only 11% of these prior enquiries, which suggests that it is perceived by these clients to have a stronger referral than direct assistance role. Whether that accurately reflects the matter or not, it is of interest to note that three-quarters of the sample were members of a public library (Table 19).

Table 19: Enquiries: membership of public library.

	Number of clients (n=76)	Total %
Yes	57	75
No	19	25

Implications

It would be invidious to suggest that some clients are more 'worthy' of help than others, since our evidence clearly indicates that clients' enquiries sprang from deeply felt and pressing motivations, whatever their particular circumstances. However, when resources are very limited, there are many who argue that they should be directed mainly to helping those with the greatest cumulative disadvantage. The difficulty lies in defining the criteria of disadvantage. All four Services have clearly attracted the unemployed, but very few clients came from the unskilled range, and most had had experience of formal education post-school, whether full-time or part-time. The Services themselves were well aware of this, and sometimes the clients were too. C1 happened also to be an adult literacy tutor who reflected from her own experience as a provider that:

...I'm quite sure that there are hundreds of people in the city who aren't aware that units like ours exist to help ordinary folk with spelling and writing letters and such. I'm quite sure there are hundreds of folk sitting at home thinking that they wish they had done it when they were children, not knowing that there really could be a future for them if they actually sought it...I would think that (Service C) was a very good referral point for people who were *looking* for courses, who *know* that there are qualifications that they might get, or who recognise that the CAT or poly or the university might be for *them*.

This statement directly reflects American experience:

Our studies and our instincts tell us that there are many more adult learners out there whom we could benefit, many more than we have reached thus far. This may be related to the newness of the idea, but we feel there are still deeper problems here, with serious implications for the whole brokering function...specifically, we are faced with two barriers: people's capacity to *hear* our message, and their ability to *respond* to our message. The first one is a matter of information processing skills, and to some degree may be resolvable. The second is almost a matter of social psychology or cultural norms, and may be very difficult to modify.[34]

Thus we underline the point on which many Services are in agreement, that attracting those with the greatest cumulative disadvantage is likely to require different long-term strategies, which in current practice may stretch the Services' meagre resources, especially demands on staff, beyond tolerable limits.

At the same time, it is perfectly clear that Services are already serving clienteles who badly need the assistance they offer and many would fit into the category of 'disadvantaged'. The effects of Services' various outreach strategies are interesting. Service A had attended carefully to the leafleting of its Job Centre and attracted 25% of its sample in this way; Service B had profited from a local radio broadcast (70% of the sample); Service C had the liaison with its central library (45%); and Service D's shop-front was itself an outreach strategy. From the limited perspective of our client sample, attracting disadvantaged clients appears to depend less on the location of the Service than on the forms of outreach adopted. For example, Service C attracted the largest proportion of clients with exposure to higher education and also the largest proportion of library-referred clients. Our parallel study of central libraries' educational enquirers shows them to be more likely to be high-educated and in professional employment than the typical EGSA enquirer, which may therefore account for this feature of Service C's client profile. There were certainly fewer differences among the clients attracted by Service A (located in the Careers Advisory Service office), Service B (located in a central library but largely recruiting from outside) and Service D, in high-street shop-front premises. We cannot say whether similar conclusions may be drawn about EGSAs located in educational establishments — though it is noted (Table 18) that 28% of prior enquiries made by clients were to educational institutions.

The extent to which both clients and advisers perceive educational enquiries to overlap with employment opportunities is also significant. This has important implications for the Services, relationships with those agencies that offer specialist help and for the Services staff's own training in this area. In such circumstances, the closure of, Occupational Guidance Units and the widespread retrenchment of the Careers Advisory Service towards a concentration on the sixteen–nineteen years age group is of particular concern.

More generally, it is clear that Services have major problems in making themselves and their facilities known to the large number of institutions and agencies who may deal with clients likely to profit from educational guidance. Services' limited success with such outreach may result in haphazard referral and/or a process of self-selection, whereby those clients who are most determined and most articulate will present themselves. Service D is the exception, here, with its high-street 'drop-in' premises. Even so, a weakness in reaching potential consumers who do not happen to pass down that street was apparent to clients as well as to advisers. As D15 commented, 'I haven't seen them publicised, I've never heard of them, it was just by chance that I saw it'. Redressing this problem is a complex issue for all our Services.

CHAPTER SEVEN
THE ADVISER/CLIENT INTERACTION

The next five chapters draw primarily on data from the interviews conducted with clients and advisers, supported by evidence from the ratings scales administered to both parties. The material is discussed under headings of assessment, information, advice and counselling, referral and implementation. Clients were followed-up at an appropriate time after their interview at the EGSA and this data provides the basis for the last section.

The broad nature of the enquiries, as perceived by client and adviser separately, is shown in Table 15 and discussed in Chapter 6. The normal length of interviews between clients and advisers varied greatly. At Services A and B, most interviews were conducted to a pre-determined time and might last half an hour or an hour. At Service C, interactions were quite short, often only a few minutes; and most were conducted by telephone. At Service D, there was no pre-determined time limit.

Table 20 shows the aspects of the interview on which advisers estimated most time was spent. Sometimes advisers felt that more than one aspect predominated; and in one-third of cases, they were unable to analyse the interview in this way. Nevertheless, the Table provides a guide to the disposition of time to specific elements of the guidance process. Again there were substantial variations between Services, particularly for information. Service C estimated this aspect to predominate in seventeen (85%) of its cases; Service D in seven (44%) of cases; and Services A and B in only three (15%) of cases. Service C perceived assessment to predominate in five (25%) of cases, compared with none for Service D. Service C also accounted for six of the instances of predominance of implementation. Figures for advice and counselling have been aggregated, since advisers often found these elements difficult to disentangle, but the proportions were approximately the same for each Service.

Table 20: EGSA interviews: aspects of interview on which advisers estimated most time was spent

Aspect	Number of interviews where most time devoted to this (n=76)	Total interviews %
Assessment	9	12
Information	30	39
Advice and counselling	17	22
Implementation	8	11
No answer	25	33

CHAPTER EIGHT
ASSESSMENT

Introduction
Our preliminary discussions with the four Services showed that assessment was not perceived as a central part of the assistance offered to clients. It was generally understood as gathering factual details about the clients' background, supplemented with discussion about their aspirations and so on. Only one Service (Service D) commented on the potential value of independent testing facilities for some clients. This chapter examines the amount and type of assessment; the conduct of the assessment process; and some implications for practice.

Amount and type of assessment
Table 21 shows the number and proportions of clients being assessed on each main attribute, as reported by advisers and clients. From the viewpoint of the advisers, the Table shows considerable variation in the frequency with which the various attributes were taken into consideration. For example, clarification of the client's current qualifications arose with fifty-five (72%) clients; assessment of potentialities with only twenty (26%) clients. There was also wide variation among the four Services. The first four attributes, which may collectively be termed the client's personal circumstances, were considered with broadly equal attention by Services A and B. Service C assessed the financial circumstances of only one client; made the lowest number of assessments of clients' personality (five); but included assessment of clients' physical circumstances in no less than seventeen cases. Service D's assessments fell between Service C's and those of Services A and B. Again there was broad agreement among Services A, B and D that the majority of clients were assessed in the 'education' and 'work' categories; but only two clients were assessed on their educational background at Service C, which also made the lowest number of assessments of work background. According to the advisers' viewpoint, abilities were assessed in at least 60% of cases at Services A, B and D but in only two (10%) cases at Service C. Clients' potentialities received little attention at any Service except for Service B (fourteen clients), perhaps because of its emphasis on counselling. This Service also examined the motivations of its clients most frequently. These findings match with Service C's self-description as essentially an information and referral agency, involving short interactions conducted by telephone; and with Services A, B and D's greater emphasis on advice and counselling. With regard to assessment of potentialities, Services A, C and D saw this aspect of assessment as

one for course providers to offer clients, rather than the Service itself. As an example, D11 was enquiring about social work courses and the adviser commented on her potential thus:

...I think it is very difficult in a lot of cases for us to say, 'Oh, that person, she couldn't get there'. I mean, I would like her to have every opportunity to explore the course of action that we were talking about, in the hope that she can get in there...because I do think she'll make an ideal social worker.

D11 was consequently sent to the appropriate course tutor for further discussions. This Service was also the only one which appeared to engage in dialogue with relevant course tutors about the potential of the client referred. Thus, in discussion of D2, a Service D adviser commented:

...(D2) would go to the class and see the tutor and then I would take up with...the tutor concerned what he feels this person is going to do and that would lead into other options that we might discuss at a later date...I would hope it would be an on-going process...

Table 21: EGSA interviews: number and proportions of clients being assessed on each main attribute, as reported by advisers and clients

Attribute assessed	Adviser		Client	
	Number of clients (n=76)	Total %	Number of clients (n=76)	Total %
Family circumstances	40	53	15	20
Financial circumstances	30	39	16	21
Personality	43	57	11	14
Physical circumstances	36	47	29	38
Educational background	34	45	29	38
Qualifications	55	72	35	46
Work experience	39	51	30	39
Current work status	50	66	28	37
Abilities	41	54	17	22
Potentialities	20	26	6	8
Motivations	49	64	17	22
Aspirations	38	50	29	38

Table 21 shows that clients were much less likely than advisers to perceive assessments as having taken place. Agreement between advisers' and clients' perceptions was highest for the attributes of physical circumstances, educational background, work experience and aspirations, where there was coincidence of views in about three-quarters of cases. Agreement was lowest for the attributes of personality, potentialities and motivations, where coincidence of views was one-third or less. The largest total discrepancy was at Service A, where advisers reported three times as many assessments as clients; the lowest was at Service C, where advisers reported

Table 22: EGSA interviews: mean number of attributes assessed as reported by advisers and clients

Mean number of attributes in which assessment was made

EGSA	Adviser perceived	Client perceived
A	7.3	2.6
B	7.7	5.3
C	4.0	3.0
D	5.9	2.9

Table 23: EGSA interviews: attributes assessed in order of frequency of assessment, according to advisers' and clients' perceptions

Advisers	Number of clients assessed	Clients	Number of clients assessed
Educational qualifications	55	Educational qualifications	35
Current work status	50	Work experience	30
Motivations	49	Educational background	29
Personality	43	Aspirations	29
Abilities	41	Physical circumstances	29
Family circumstances	40	Current work status	28
Work experience	39	Abilities	17
Aspirations	38	Motivations	17
Physical circumstances	36	Financial circumstances	16
Educational background	34	Family circumstances	15
Financial circumstances	30	Personality	11
Potentialities	20	Potentialities	6

Table 24: EGSA interviews: method of assessment

	Adviser		Client	
Method	Number of instances of this	Total %	Number of instances of this	Total %
Requested	33	15	36	36
Intuited	86	40	9	9
Volunteered	93	44	54	54
Instruments	1	(1)	1	1
TOTAL	213	100	140	100

approximately 25% more assessments than clients. Table 22 shows the differences between Services in the mean number of attributes assessed. Table 23 shows clearly the differences between advisers' and clients' perceptions of the frequency of the various attributes of assessment.

Some of these discrepancies may of course be explained by both parties' misremembering certain elements in the transaction. A stronger explanation lies in the way in which these assessments were reached. Both advisers and clients were asked during our interviews whether the assessment was obtained by a question from the adviser, was volunteered by the client, was intuited or was obtained by the use of an objective tool of measurement. Table 24 shows (wherever such ascriptions could reliably be made) that advisers' intuition was used almost as much as data volunteered by the client, but that clients remained largely unaware of this intuitive element in the assessment process. This factor was clearly present at all the Services, but was most marked, both in amount (forty-five instances) and in clients' limited awareness (two instances) at Service B.

Conduct of the assessment process
The approach to assessment most commonly adopted was to ask clients one or two general questions about their enquiry and to request some basic personal information. Clients' responses were typically to volunteer more information about themselves, on which advisers could base their initial assessment. This was supplemented and perhaps modified by information generated during the course of the interview. This approach is illustrated by the comments of Service D adviser on D5:

> ...the question 'Can I ask how old you are?'... that opens up the field...the position regarding fees, time you've been out of work — you can get reduced fees...and also through observation and intuition...and it was fairly obvious what his job was because he had a motor bike and all the paraphernalia that motor bike messengers have...

In no case did advisers report any systematic attempt at detailed assessment of the client before proceeding with other aspects of the interview. Facts such as educational background, work experience and aspirations were usually gathered by requested or volunteered information; and matters such as personality and potentialities by the exercise of the adviser's intuition. In only one case was a standard instrument used. This arose with C3, who was referred to an adviser for counselling, rather than for extra information or enrolment. She was offered Open University materials for working out career and life plans, which the adviser's employment enabled him to have to hand.

Advisers generally (though there were exceptions, particularly at Service B) took clients largely at their self-evaluation:

...you have to take some basic facts on face value. Otherwise, it's half-an-hour trying to find out information if you've really got to start at the beginning and say are you really very good at that and so on. (Adviser, Service A)

This was said to be a result both of lack of time and of the necessary expertise to make more objectified assessments; certainly some advisers recognised the problems of self-evaluation. But some clients were not considered to need a more thorough assessment: there were scruples about intruding too far into the client's personal domain. As a Service A adviser put it:

...I think, if people want you to know, that they'll tell you straight away. They volunteer the information.

For Service C, the telephone was felt to contribute its own inhibitions:

...I think no matter how skilled you are you never get a correct idea of people on the telephone. I think you have got to see them face to face and discuss the matter. (Adviser, Service C)

This viewpoint was echoed by several Service C clients, such as C14 who said:

...Maybe if I had come to the office it might have been better. Maybe I would have asked more. When you're on the 'phone you tend to forget things that you need to ask;

or C15 who felt no accurate assessment of her could have been made because:

...I don't think you can unless you meet someone, just sitting and talking to someone over the 'phone.

Even within the confines of the self-evaluation assessment, our evidence suggests three main problems. One was a sometimes limited knowledge of the options raised by clients. This was picked up by clients themselves during their interviews with us:

...I think under the circumstances really she made as much of an assessment as I needed. I suppose on the other hand if she had known a bit more about universities and degree courses she possibly could have told me whether I should go ahead with the application and whether I would be qualified to get in. (B20)

...I think at one stage he mentioned something about an association up X Town way to teach English to Asian people, and I wasn't sure whether he had misunderstood me then, that perhaps he thought I wanted to teach English to these people, but I wanted to do the actual course, to get the diploma at the end to be qualified to teach English to foreign students. (C5)

The second was that sometimes even the most essential factual assessment was not collected or not fully understood by the adviser and so did not inform the range of options suggested. For example, B6, who was unemployed, was recommended to a course some distance away — the adviser assuming he was a member of a wage-earning family. During his interview with us the client explained why he had disregarded this option:

It's the bus fare. I get unemployment benefit — when I pay the rent, £15 rent, I've got nothing left. What about the food? That's the problem, that's what I tried to explain to her.

Sometimes this rather haphazard approach to collecting necessary information was caused by a desire to present a relaxed and informal environment in which the client could feel at ease. As a Service D adviser commented:

> ...I think there are ways of getting people to provide additional information — partly by the way you present yourself to them — if you can do it in an informal way...I try...to make people feel relaxed when they come in.

The third was that assessments of the more concrete or tangible aspects of the client's life were, as we have earlier noted, sometimes supplemented by intuitive judgements unverified with clients. As a Service D adviser commented:

> ...I think you do pick things up through non-verbal communication...and you can to some extent make judgments as to whether or not the person feels that this is suitable for them and whether or not they have any anxieties and self-doubt about what you're suggesting...

Both the extent and the nature of these intuitions could be substantial. For example, a Service B adviser intuited from a client's school and work background thus:

> (Have you checked up on his educational background?)
> ...Not too closely — he hadn't any qualifications, he'd no CSEs or 'O' levels or anything like that, so I didn't press that too far. He was obviously a practical man, but even so he needs some ability in English and some Maths, but he seemed quite confident and he seemed as if he could manage, he could take care of himself, he was obviously a man that if he didn't know how to do anything he would find out, and if he had difficulties with it on the academic side he would get help.
> (Why did you feel that about him?)
> ...In the course of the conversation, because of what he had done previously. We were sort of talking about his work background and what he had done, so that...I mean he was apprentice trained, so they have to have a fair amount of gumption to do that, haven't they? I felt that he would be all right.

It is evident that such intuited assessments could have far-reaching influence on the course of the Service transaction and on the value of the outcome for the client. Two examples illustrate this point. Client A9 had previously abandoned a university course (in a quite different field) after failing Part 1 finals and, after a recent job dismissal, was now seeking a second chance in higher education. The adviser's summation of the client, based on such background information, was 'I think he was a non-starter really'. Although the adviser provided A9 with information on a number of courses and encouraged him to apply, she commented:

> ...I didn't go into the problem of his financial situation because I think that he would have difficulty in getting in anyway.

Follow-up revealed that A9 had experienced no difficulty whatsoever in being accepted on four of the courses to which he applied. However, he did encounter great difficulty in obtaining grant aid and was obliged in the end to abandon his hopes of a degree. This is a case where more accurate appraisal of the user's potential might have led to provision of adequate information on grant eligibility. This would at least have prevented a sudden disappointment in the face of success in being accepted on the course and might have led to alternative ways back into education.

In the case of C8, enquiring about studying Norwegian, an inference was drawn by the adviser thus:

...My impression on the 'phone was she was a fairly well educated person, she was certainly very enthusiastic,

and a recommendation was made accordingly that she make contact with a language laboratory to pursue some linguistic studies. However, in interview, client C8 declared herself to be very nervous, lacking in confidence and possessing only three CSEs, so she felt she could not use this option as she very much desired tutor contact and a group atmosphere. The only other option offered to her she had failed to understand.

Some of these examples indicate clearly that intuitive assessments are based as much on the attitudes of the adviser as they are on the cues given by the client. It appeared to us that advisers were sometimes quite unconscious of their personal impact on the assessment process and that they perceived their assessments to be sufficiently accurate for them to deal adequately with the enquiry. At Service C, for example, discussion of family and financial circumstances took place only in cases of female clients where changes in domestic circumstances or financial dependence made them obviously relevant. Such considerations were apparently not seen as relevant in male cases, even though male clients C17 and C19 proved to be financially dependent upon parents, while client C18's decision to change career was linked to recent marriage guidance and client C20 was preparing for retirement.

Sometimes advisers' attitudes were very conscious ones, which powerfully informed the process of their transactions with clients. While it is not inappropriate for advisers to hold strong views, there are dangers when such matters are not fully communicated to clients. As an example, one of the advisers at Service B saw two women clients during the research and made the same assessment of them both, based on her belief that women always underestimated their capabilities:

...(This client) neither said, 'No, I'm not capable, I cannot do that' — or if she knew she wasn't capable she did say, 'I don't think that will be suitable for me'...I think at the beginning of the interview she was aiming rather

90

low for herself — a lot of this age group don't tend to assess themselves very highly.

(Why — what did she say?)

...It was more her attitude than what she said — 'I'm not a very clever sort of person but can you do anything for me'. After discussion I think she blossomed out and had a little more regard for herself. I think women on the whole do tend to rate themselves very low. I feel rather sad about that — I don't think they should because when a woman is doing one job and is going to attempt to do another — a married woman who is running her own home — I think she has quite a bit of ability there.

(Did you ask her about any previous jobs?)

...Yes — I think she had done factory work and things like that — textiles — they were very ordinary jobs — they were more craft than mental but I see no reason why she couldn't manage a little mental one — a little more mental ability on her part would really bring her up to be able to do something.

This client, B17, actually wanted a change of job, but she followed the advice given and went on to a Return to Study course, which she neither enjoyed nor completed. As a result she returned to a job as a sewing machinist which, in her interview with us, she had declared she did not wish to do. She said of the course, when followed up:

...I think I got hold of the wrong end of the stick. I thought it was to try out different jobs...

It was not always the case that advisers dealt with client assessment on a self-assessment basis; and there were occasions when particular aspects of the intuitive process were checked with clients. However, it appears generally that the approach to assessment adopted by the four Services worked best for those who knew clearly what they required, could convey this articulately and present the relevant personal information, *or* for those who were honest enough to say they had little idea of where they were heading. For those who could not confidently assess themselves or who came for guidance with a 'presenting problem', there was no guarantee that this would be perceived. We have noted earlier that this problem provides one explanation of the discrepancy between advisers' and clients' perceptions of the broad nature of the enquiry (Table 15). As client C17 reflected in retrospect:

...In the first place I had my mind made up about what was the right thing to do, the sort of thing I wanted in adult education and he might have felt that this person seems to know what he wants and we'll just give him the information, as simple as that. If I'd been a bit vague and not known what I really wanted, he might have asked some questions and been able to determine more as to my situation then.

However, even where clients came only with a stated aim of wanting to do something, to make a change, there were problems. In these cases, advisers usually secured more background information about the client, but this tended to be gathered unsystematically (through adopting a 'listening' stance) and was based on information selected by the client. Although clients of this type often reported in interview that they were pleased to have had someone listen to them, they were also likely to express disappointment at being no further on.

When clients were aware of being assessed, we found no evidence that clients objected to being scrutinised, even when the adviser pressed quite hard. As B16 commented:

> ...He seemed very careful, a very meticulous man, he was going over...there was one or two things he covered twice, like, just to make sure I suppose to himself...I think actually one of the reasons he was a bit firm with me was to make sure I was serious about doing further education.

Indeed, while advisers might intuit that clients were reluctant to discuss personal matters, in their interviews with us these clients most usually did so spontaneously. Several expressed disappointment at the lack of more detailed analysis of their needs and circumstances. As an example, C18, who was offered no assessment (or counselling) to establish the reality of his aspiration to take up computing as a career, commented:

> ...I thought he would have probed me a little bit to see if I was any good on this point or that point, and then advise me a little bit. I mean, I came in with this half-baked notion of going into computers somewhere along the line...I thought there would have been someone to have said, well, you had better go on a maths course before you go there, something of that nature...I didn't want to waste money going on a course where people were talking and it was going over my head, or, on the other hand, learning with just shop assistants or people who were doing it for a night out.

And D15, commenting on the limited assessment (apparently) of her skills and abilities, illuminated some clients' tendency to blame themselves:

> ...No, not really, I hoped he would. He didn't ask me what subjects or anything...I think he just thought I was going to extend my nursing, but that is maybe partly my fault...

Implications

In Chapter 3 we noted that three conditions were needed to provide adequate assessment. These were first, access to an appropriately trained assessor; second, that assessment should be bias-free; third, that the assessor should be adequately informed about educational opportunities available in the area. Our evidence suggests that the training some advisers had had did little to prepare them for the complex problems presented to them. We do not refer here to the specific professional competences required to administer standard psychological tests, although we believe that some clients would have benefited from such facilities; but to the area of adjudging the context of the client in a systematic way. The haphazard manner in which many assessments were made is itself an uncomfortable finding, but even more so is the fact that so much was made in an unconscious way and thus hidden from the clients. The omission of highly pertinent detail and the exercise of advisers' biases could — and did — adversely affect the process of the interview and its value for the clients. This was further exacerbated by some advisers' limited knowledge, both in range and depth, of available options.

The need for systematisation and training is apparent, as is consideration of ways in which assessment can be opened up, that is, made apparent to and shared with clients. This matter is important for two reasons. First, it may help to make assessments more valid. Second, it may obviate the danger of systematised assessments appearing threatening, over-formal or depersonalised to the client. It would be overstating the case to claim that all clients suffered from incomplete consideration of relevant data about them or that all intuitive assessments were inaccurate. But the point remains that by present methods advisors cannot be certain that they have taken all pertinent detail into account; and clients may be left with some insecurity.

Reliance on self-assessment does offer advisers the chance to avoid areas of delicate consideration (for example, the client's financial circumstances); and the same applies to intuitive judgments based on clients' presentation of themselves (for example, their personality). Information requested by advisers tended to relate to more concrete or tangible aspects of an individual's life, but even so was dependent on the client's ability to convey all the relevant detail. This placed a heavy onus of responsibility on clients who were not sure what exactly they should offer, how they should behave, or exactly what the EGSA could provide. As D15 remarked:

> ...you see I didn't know what the actual 'shop' as it were, was about. I thought they just gave out leaflets, I didn't know, I just saw this thing, and I thought, 'Well, is it school-leavers, or what?' I didn't know what it was for, and was too nervous really to ask, and then I was approached, which I thought was very helpful. Then I suppose I wasn't actually asked exactly what I wanted, and I didn't really get down to it. I didn't realise what their job was.

Evidence indicates that educational guidance is a cluster, not a linear, process, so that assessment will affect even 'simple' information provision as well as the other functions of educational guidance. This point was confirmed in our study of librarians' activity and suggests that EGSAs need to attend not only to the awareness training and diagnostic skills of their full advisory staff, but also to that of 'first-line' assisters, such as clerical staff. At Service D, this matter appears less important than at Services A and B, since the clerical or other assistant's role was carefully controlled and there was almost always an adviser on hand. Where these circumstances do not apply, particular dangers may arise from over-reliance on the client's knowledge base — and hence their ability to ask the right questions. It is notable that all our Services considered that the 'leisure' enquiry might be dealt with adequately by untrained staff, but even this appears to be an assumption open to question, in view of the links apparent with vocational aspirations. We do not argue that all 'information-only' enquiries necessarily imply a greater guidance need, only that it is not a simple matter to predict which do and which do not need further assistance.

We note that EGSAs may rely in some instances on the competence of contacts — usually course tutors — to assess clients' suitability for particular options. While this procedure may well be appropriate, it raises the question (already considered in Chapter 5) of the precise role of such contacts and the extent to which they can fulfil the task demanded of them. It also leaves unresolved the question of who is ultimately responsible for the general assessment of the client's potential. As a final point on assessment, we found that a few clients were subject to assessment procedures in the form of entrance examinations, but only one, D5, was forewarned and prepared for this.

CHAPTER NINE

INFORMATION

Introduction

The provision of educational information was an essential feature of educational guidance for all four Services taking part in the research. However, Services varied in both the amount and the type of information provided directly, depending on their perceptions of their role. This chapter examines the approach to educational information adopted by each Service; the conduct of information provision during the adviser/client interviews; some particular problems and successes; and implications for practice.

In considering this function of educational guidance, we were aware that it was not only in itself a complex process, but that it was intermixed with assessment, advice, counselling and implementation in ways deeply important for individual clients. This is clearly portrayed in the description of information-based needs of unemployed clients in Service B's sample, which is quoted here in full:

...1. There are those people who desparately need a job. They are short of money, angry and very bitter. Information about what is available is not enough. People in this position have a need for long-term assistance if they are to find help through education.

2. There are people who are unemployed and perhaps accept their position as a temporary one lasting as long as the recession. They wish to use the time now available to them to 'improve themselves'. Many people return to 'unfinished business', to master the skills they wish they had learnt at school.

3. There are people who want a training which will give them a skill for which there is a need in society, i.e. with a job at the end of the course. They are asking for specialised information which to a certain degree is guesswork or future projection. They can be given information about available vocational courses: availability of such courses often means that those pursuing it are likely to be employed at the end. Here again these people need long-term assistance. Many of them will fail the entrance exams for TOPS courses, since rising numbers means rising standards: at that point they will need more help and information. Some courses give students an opportunity to try out various jobs at the same time as basic learning skills are being improved. Unfortunately such courses are rare and therefore oversubscribed.

4. Some people want to learn a specific skill, sometimes because they have been offered a job if they have that particular skill or because they wish to start a business on their own. The information they need is not to be found in prospectuses but by *personal contact* with the relevant tutors running related courses.

5. There are those who have already been well educated and trained for a particular job only to find that at the end of the training there are no jobs available. Often a major problem is the financial aspect since second grants are not available. Their particular experiences are salutory for those returning to education and those who give them advice and information.

6. There are women who are unemployed because their children have gone to school. The most common request from these women is that they do not want to return to the boring jobs they did before they had children. Because women are still responsible for their children out of school hours and pre-school children, their information needs are very specific, e.g. creche facilities and costs, start and finish times.

Approaches to educational information

At the time of our research, Service A's approach to the information function was to provide its clients with 'basic' information, that is, to draw together public-level information about continuing education in the area. This was done primarily from a collection of institutions' prospectuses and from information sheets on modes of provision. It was also beginning to devise a card-index of courses by subject and had immediate access to the Careers Advisory Service's personnel and library. This library contained a wide range of careers materials and a small collection of continuing education directories. Service A did not view itself as a complete information-provider, because of what it perceived to be the devolved nature of much educational information. Emphasis was placed instead on the Service's networks to supplement public-level materials.

It appeared to us that the Service's low-resource operational approach, as well as more theoretical matters, had largely formed its attitude to information provision, with limited finances, borrowed premises, and a busy volunteer workforce as important contributory factors. This underlined the importance of backup from the Careers Advisory Service, with advisers especially appreciative of its library and of the expertise of particular officers.

Service B's attitude to its role in information provision was very different. The Service had from its inception envisaged the collection, storage and retrieval of educational information as a task large and complex enough to warrant computerisation. We have noted in Chapter 5 that its experimentation in this field was not entirely successful from the point of view of immediate use by the Service, though it did succeed in testing a system which might ultimately provide both an index and a browsing facility. The Service's decision to locate itself within the public library also reflected the value of access to that library's excellent materials collection and the bibliographical expertise of its senior staff.

The materials considered essential for Service B's activities were selected after consultation with senior librarians, Careers Service advisers and the LEA. The library provided (and continues to provide) a collection of directories for the Service's sole use, its extensive computerised listing of clubs and societies, COIC material, and duplicates of the many individual brochures and prospectuses it receives from individual providers, locally and regionally.

The library, like most, is recognised and used by educational institutions in the city and beyond as a promotional disseminator of information and thus receives a wide range of such material. Service B's information collection therefore covered full-time and part-time courses (including correspondence courses), vocational training, voluntary work, clubs and societies, private institutions, and details of the provision of community and unemployment centres. Its emphasis was on local provision; clients needing information on national availability would have access to the host library's collection of materials.

In view of the volume of information being received and of the size of the adviser team at Service B, the role of the Service's clerical assistant was described as 'the linchpin of the communication network'. Her information duties included organising materials by filing them in the several dozen boxes used for storage; providing information to clients perceived to need 'information-only' assistance; and selecting and arranging information for advisers' use when something of the nature of the client's enquiry was known.

Service C, of the four Services taking part in our research, was the Service that placed greatest emphasis on the rapid conveyance of educational information to clients, with referral on where necessary. The aim was to provide public-level information which was as up-to-date and reliable as possible. Advisers were confident that they achieved their highest rate of success within this function. The Service's office served as a central collection of information about provision offered by linked advisers and by other institutions and agencies in the area. Its information resources were chiefly prospectuses and brochures for nearly all public institutions within the four LEAs in Service C membership; some information on provision beyond those areas; a selection of materials about private provision, correspondence courses and other agencies; and information on grants. The central library, with whom Service C had close connections, maintained an excellent collection of brochures and prospectuses, particularly for higher education provision, and an extensive array of relevant directories. Service C used this source to supplement its own collection and also made extensive use of its networked contacts for detail not contained in brochures.

The Service's own collection was filed in pigeon-holes labelled according to provider and cross-referenced on to a card index file which was in process of construction. This was intended to provide a fast-access guide to what subjects were being provided, where and by whom, and a means of enabling new staff to acclimatise themselves to local provision, though it was likely to require substantial updating each year.

Service D's approach to information provision also reflected its structure and the perceptions of its role. It appeared to differ from Services A, B and C in several important respects. First, it placed particular emphasis on the role of semi-public and especially private information in its service to clients. Much (though not all) of such information was understood to be gained from clients themselves, who were actively encouraged to revisit the Service. Second, and as a related point, it was considered inappropriate to 'overload' clients with information which might be better absorbed (and therefore acted upon) by a step-by-step approach. In any case, Service D had a guarded approach to face-value information-only enquiries. For this reason, even the informational function of the Service's clerical worker was carefully controlled. Thus the continuous presence of the same professional staff at the Service's shop were prerequisites of its general approach.

Service D's public-level information was deliberately limited by its self-perception as a very local Service, although, being situated in inner London, the volume of material to be collected, stored and retrieved did not appear to be less than for other Services. Indeed, part of the reason that Service D had been active in encouraging the development of other Services in the London area was because the lack of a network of similar Services constrained its own effective operation. Service D had developed (with the assistance of volunteers) a card index which was intended to be fully comprehensive. However, the task was discovered to be too time-consuming, so this tool now primarily covered leisure provision. Thought had been given to computerisation, but consultations had not identified a workable system for a Service with such local demand. The Service continued to feel a need for more 'rational' storage and retrieval methods, but in the meantime relied on its own ad-hoc approach. Its information collection consisted primarily of local brochures and prospectuses and London-wide material, with lesser attention to national provision and to careers information. Some correspondence course information was also retained.

Amount and type of information

Table 25 shows the number and proportions of various types of information given during the seventy-six interviews of clients that we analysed. It is clear that information is concentrated on the public sector; and that from the advisers' viewpoint, information on higher and further education is most commonly offered, accounting for well over half of all instances. Again, there were substantial differences between Services. About 33% of Service D's information was for higher education, compared with 14% at Service A. Further education accounted for about 30% of Services A, B and C's information, but only about 15% for Service D. Service B accounted for three-quarters of all instances of adult education information and the only instances of WEA/extra-mural provision.

Table 25: EGSA interviews: instances of types of information given

Type of information	Adviser		Client	
	Number of instances (n=200)	Total %	Number of instances (n=185)	Total %
University	11	6	15	8
Open University	9	5	9	5
Other higher education	31	16	33	18
WEA/extra-mural	3	2	1	1
Further education	54	27	40	22
Adult education	25	13	22	12
Basic education	10	5	8	4
Grants	13	7	19	10
Correspondence courses	6	3	3	2
Private courses	3	2	1	1
Careers information	15	8	18	10
Job Centre	10	5	10	5
Other	10	5	6	3

The ten instances only of basic education information were made (equally) by Services B and D. Services were similar in giving little information on correspondence courses (other than the Open University) and on private courses, with Service D providing no such information to its clients. Grants information also figured very little; Service D gave most, a finding in line with its higher proportion of information provision on higher education. (The discrepant figures for recall of grants information is accounted for entirely by Service D, where one adviser failed consistently to recall having given such information, while clients were quite clear she had done so). Careers information was most commonly given by Service A, reflecting its location in its local Careers Advisory Service. Information about the Job Centre and various training opportunities available through it was provided almost entirely by Service B, perhaps reflecting the vocationally-oriented nature of this particular sample. The 'Other' category instances were fairly evenly distributed between Services, and included information on voluntary work, clubs and so on. It is interesting to note that Service B advisers reported well over twice as many instances of information-giving as the other Services, which may be taken to reflect its broader information base; its policy of direct as

99

opposed to devolved information provision; its exploratory approach to interviews, with a particular emphasis on advice and counselling; and the longer time given to such inteviews than was given by the other Services. In contrast, it will be recalled that Service A saw much of its information function as devolved; Service C operated primarily by telephone; and Service D had a policy of staged information provision.

Two other matters apparent from Table 25 may be noted. The first is the apparently low level of demand for basic education courses. The second is the relatively low incidence of information provision on careers and local Job Centre opportunities. This compares uneasily with our evidence of the vocational implications of clients' enquiries (see Table 15), but reflects EGSAs' concern not to overlap with the work of specialist agencies making provision in this area. Such an approach also reduces EGSAs' own information burden, but reinforces the need for close liaison with vocational guidance provision.

Table 25 also shows clients' recall of information provision to be broadly in line with that of advisers. We feel that minor discrepancies are due to lapses of memory by both parties, but particularly by advisers who were often hard-pressed and did not record all the information provided. On the other hand, there were several instances where clients appeared to have forgotten, or failed to understand, some of the information given to them. Verbal information given during interview was most likely to suffer in this way: an important consideration since, when it was based on semi-public or even private sources, it might be more accurate and more precisely tailored to the individual than brochure details.

Table 26 shows the sources used in advisers' information searches. Brochures and prospectuses figure as the most important sources, accounting for nearly half of all usages; they were most commonly used at Service B (58%), least at Service A (30%). The Services' own materials, especially their indexes, accounted for one in five usages overall, though with wide variation between Services, dependent on the extent to which they were able to maintain the usability of such tools. Service B made most use of its own materials (26% of sources used) and Service D the least (3% of sources used). Direct use of institutions and agencies also accounted for about one in five of all sources and again wide variations were apparent. As an example, Service A made most use of Careers, which accounted for twelve out of thirteen of its total institution/agency source contacts, with the other Services making few or no approaches to them for information. Instances of the use of advisers' own knowledge were limited almost entirely to Services A and D. In the case of Service A, this was attributable to volunteers supplementing brochure information with their immediate professional expertise; all the volunteers interviewed during our research at this Service were professionally employed in continuing education. That 'Advisers' own knowledge' constituted 41% of Service D's information sources reflects its particular emphasis on semi-public and private information. Directories were uniformly little used, which was perhaps surprising in view of the relatively large numbers of enquiries with a higher education element. Service D made the point that they are expensive items to buy.

Discrepancies between advisers' and clients' recall of sources are attributable mainly to the fact that clients were unlikely to be aware of the source unless printed materials were consulted in front of them; and the search was often conducted away from the client. At Service C, for example, it was common practice for an adviser to ring back or write to a client after consulting appropriate sources. Additionally, clients were unlikely to be aware that some aspects of information were derived from advisers' own knowledge. In these respects, the Services' approach to informing their clients presents an interesting contrast with public libraries' self-help style. EGSAs appear to adopt a mediatory approach, with the adviser placed between client and information, to direct the selection and interpretation process. The links between assessment, information and advice are thus evident; furthermore, such an approach places a special responsibility on advisers to tackle the information task to the best advantage of the client.

Table 26: EGSA interviews: information sources used

	Adviser		Client	
Source	Number of instances of usage (n=206)	Total %	Number of instances of usage (n=114)	Total %
Brochures and prospectuses	92	45	76	67
EGSAs own materials	39	19	17	15
Institutions and agencies	38	18	11	10
Advisers' own knowledge	30	15	6	5
Directories	7	3	4	4

Conduct of information provision: some problems and successes
In broad terms, Service A's approach to information during the client interview was to array information from brochures and prospectuses, supplemented by the advisers' own professional knowledge and by heavy use of the Careers Advisory Service's library and personnel. In general such limitations as were perceived by these advisers were not regarded as particularly important:

...perhaps the Service isn't really sufficiently expert, but at least we know how to put them on to the next stage...at least I've been able to refer them to someone else.

Service B's approach was apparently much more broadly-based, so that clients were exposed to a larger range of educational options. Brochures and prospectuses were supplemented by information from the Service's own materials; other agencies were little consulted. Service B's role was less a quick-information provider than an integration of information with its advice and counselling roles. Service C aimed to provide a rapid response to specific information requests usually made by telephone. Use of outside sources was directed almost entirely to the Service's links in educational institutions. Service D concentrated its information provision within the statutory sector and gave more information on grants. Advisers' own knowledge was the prime source used, followed closely by brochures and prospectuses. Clients were deliberately not exposed to an array of information which might be too wide or too detailed to comprehend at one time and were commonly invited to digest the details given, or to pursue a particular matter, and then to call back to the Service.

During our interviews with advisers and clients, a number of common and some Service-specific problems and successes were noted. These are considered below.

A. *Comprehensive information.* There was no doubt that clients at all four Services appreciated the value of a centralised information resource, which saved them time and frustrations in their information search. As C5 commented:

> ...I was expecting perhaps even a telephonist or a general enquiry office where they'd have to put me through to a department, you know, when you have to tell your story about 1000 times, but he (the adviser) seemed to understand straight away what I was after, and he seemed to be able to help me straight away, which was unusual.

This centralisation of information was also seen by advisers to be very valuable for their clients. However, in several important respects, the information banks which had been developed were not comprehensive. Services had collected as much information as they could on the courses of the major educational institutions in their locality, but even so there were gaps in coverage. The main problem appeared to be a lack of enthusiasm by some institutions to send their brochures and prospectuses. As Service D commented:

> ...I think we find it quite difficult to get the information immediately to us. I think first of all it's because we're probably a strange animal to a lot of providers...we ask specifically for a certain number of prospectuses and in the majority of cases providers seem to ignore the fact that you are making a request for a specific number — they send you one. Also...you may get a full-time prospectus but you don't necessarily get the part-time special courses information.

Service D's problem was echoed by the other Services. A limited

102

number of prospectuses — perhaps only one — caused problems when clients needed material to take away with them, or if the Service wished to store its information in more than one mode, perhaps by subject and by institution. Lack of notification of new courses, not announced in the institution's main prospectus, meant that advisers could not be certain, without checking directly with the provider, whether they had informed clients of all the relevant courses.

When a Service did check, it often proved very profitable. For example, in the case of C1 who was seeking TEFL qualifications, details were given from a prospectus of the one-year part-time evening course, but telephone contact with the providing institution produced the additional information that a short course was proposed for an earlier date to cater for an overspill from last year's enrolment, and the client was offered the option of attending a preliminary meeting with a view to entering the earlier course if it appeared suitable.

We have already noted that the four Services defined their geo-graphical reach quite tightly, though specific definitions varied. Service A confined itself largely to the city boundaries; Service C covered four LEAs. There was some evidence that coverage was best within the immediate LEA and that outlying areas were less well attended to. Enquiries were, on the whole, local, however the locality was defined; but there was a persistent minority of clients, interested particularly in higher education, who were mobile and for whom a better range of directories might have been helpful. Only Services C and D expressed concern about being au fait with local public transport systems, so that the nearest centre identified was also the most conveniently reached.

All four Services faced problems in providing information that was prospective as well as current. The major difficulty arose during the summer months, when institutions were closed for the vacation and were unlikely to have information available on the new session's courses before late August or even early September. Moreover, the current year's materials might well be out-of-date within a few weeks of publication of prospectuses and directories might be so at or before publication. None of the Services were given advance information even of major new courses planned for one or two sessions ahead. So the importance of fostering reliable contacts within educational institutions, who might provide such information informally, was very apparent.

Table 25 showed that according to the advisers, only 5% of information provision was concerned with correspondence courses (other than the Open University) and with courses available at private institutions; and a further 5% with clubs, voluntary societies and the like (included in the category 'Other'). This limited provision of information on possible range and mode of studying in part reflected the type of clients and their stated needs, but it also reflected the limited information base of these EGSAs. Only Service B, for example, had ready access to a comprehensive listing of clubs and societies. An antipathy towards private sector provision was also apparent:

> ...We're a little reluctant because of the fact that we're not here to advertise the commercial concerns, but where it is obvious that the local authority or an educational institution can't offer a facility, then we can suggest perhaps the name and address of a commercial concern, making it quite plain that there's no guarantee. (Service C Adviser)

> ...We don't really look at private colleges, mainly because we have enough concern about what is going on in the public sector without bothering about what profit-making establishments will be doing...the few people who I have seen here have had a very bad deal out of it. I do tend to make that point...(Service D Adviser)

These matters pointed up some clients' regret that they were not offered a wider range of information. However, provision of information in depth was the single most important concern voiced by advisers *and* the area which most often disappointed clients. From the advisers' viewpoint, information provided in brochures and prospectuses too often failed to give the most elementary detail such as costs, creche facilities, transport and class times. This matter was of particular importance in view of the heavy reliance on brochures and prospectuses evidenced in Table 26. Service C, because of its specific structure and role, paid consistent attention to checking such details with the institutions themselves, and relaying this amended information to clients, by whom it was much appreciated. Service D provided a similar quality of service, except that it was less likely to check brochure information on clients' behalf by telephone: its advisers had acquired substantial knowledge of the kinds of courses locally to whom they most often referred clients. The two other Services were much more likely to rely on clients checking such detail for themselves. At Service A, for example, only one telephone call was made to check information on behalf of a client during the period of the research.

Perhaps even more critical was the confirmation we found that knowledge of semi-public information was essential to identifying the most appropriate course to meet a client's current competence and circumstances. Indeed, prospectus information might actually be misleading. As a Service D adviser commented:

> ...'Normally' — that's a very key word (in entry requirements) and to most people it's just another word — I think it should be in letters a foot high just so that people aren't automatically put off.

Strategies to deal with this difficulty varied between and within Services. Service A generally viewed provision of semi-public information of this kind as the responsibility of the referral point recommended. Service B had a large team of advisers, some of whom checked such information directly on behalf of the clients; others did not view their responsibilities in this way. Sometimes, at both A and B, taking such action depended on the time of the interview, and whether it coincided with institutions' opening times. Service C was, as we have noted, very assiduous in checking public-level information; it also checked semi-public information. This task was most usually devolved to those with specific expertise, drawn from the network of linked advisers, and the information was then relayed to clients. However, even with a well developed network of advisers, this approach could still cause problems.

> ...It has been officially approved that there will be a Service C adviser for somewhere but the people who actually matter might not have heard of you, or if they have heard of you it's a notice on the wall, but they've actually never come into contact with you, and they are not very sure that you are an official body. You could be a voluntary organisation, there's a lot, they are not quite sure what they should tell you or they shouldn't.

Service D perceived itself to be very alert to this area of information provision and enjoyed, uniquely among the four Services, information from the clients' viewpoint too. It was standard practice at this Service to supplement brochure information with semi-public information drawn from client sources as well as from the personal contacts fostered with key individuals, especially course tutors, in local educational institutions.

B. *Accurate information.* These difficulties of access to semi-public information are closely linked to the provision of accurate information. The plain fact is that the picture portrayed in public information may be very different from the actuality, so that where advisers do not seek semi-public information, the consequences for the client may be dire, especially since advisers sometimes considered the information they provided was quite adequate and so did not refer clients to further sources of assistance. Problems appeared to be particularly acute in the areas of entrance requirements, actual as opposed to publicised course availability and the approach or style of the course. Some examples may illustrate these points.

(i) One of Service B's advisers telephoned a local college during the period of our research and found that skills courses advertised in the college brochure as being for persons employed in particular trades were open now to the unemployed and that the course fee charged was nominal. The following week the adviser saw another client; because he had this semi-public information he was able to direct the client to one of these courses. However, a different adviser who interviewed a client wanting to learn welding informed the client that the courses at the college were only for people in employment. Client B5 commented:

> ...Seemingly all the courses, or the biggest part of the courses, the most comprehensive courses, you had to be in full employment anyway which struck me off immediately. It didn't strike me as being particularly sensible, being the restriction on people who are unemployed, I can't

understand that at all. You would think that people who were unemployed, trying to learn a new trade or skill, especially if you ended up with some sort of diploma or certificate at the end of it, would use the course more than people who were in full time employment.

(ii) A10 was very disappointed after telephoning colleges about several of the courses suggested to him by the adviser, to be told he either did not possess the relevant entrance qualifications or there were no vacant places on the course:

> ...I think they should perhaps look into the information they've got as far as applicants for various courses go and then they can actually inform the people while they're actually at the interview whether they're going to be able to get on these courses or not. And whether there's any places left.

was the suggestion he afterwards made.

(iii) A19, initially very pleased with the information given during interview, had at the time of follow-up abandoned the 'A' level course for which she had registered because she (a) found the other students to be considerably younger than herself, and (b) the schoolroom methods of teaching were quite unsuited to her needs. By this time, it was too late to find an alternative class.

On the other hand, we have noted that some Services/advisers did successfully pursue such semi-public information. As an example, in the case of C6, who was seeking information about courses in nutrition and catering, it was possible to supplement information provided in print with the knowledge that there was likely to be little stress put on formal entrance requirements if the client interviewed well.

Problems in the handling of semi-public information were exacerbated by Services' failure to record such information, for use by other advisers with other clients. This mattered little at Service D, where there were only two permanent advisory staff, who worked closely with each other. At Service C, however, centre advisers' knowledge was likely to disappear with them when their appointment was temporary, only to be slowly and laboriously re-established by new members of staff. At Services A and B, this procedural lapse was even more significant, staffed as they were by numbers of volunteers, who might well be able to give only two or three hours a week to the Service, and who only met occasionally with their colleagues.

Accuracy was not only prejudiced however, in the matter of semi-public information. On a public level, and bearing in mind the deficiencies in brochures and prospectuses noted earlier, some advisers were occasionally tempted into guesswork about provision; and there were occasional instances where advisers had serious misunderstandings and confusions which they relayed as actual fact to clients. More commonly, there were some areas of public-level information which were not considered the province of the Service because the information was too difficult or too vast to deal with. Much of careers and training information, perhaps understandably, came within this category. Surprisingly, grants information was often treated in the same way, not by Service D but by the other Services. As one Service C adviser put it:

> ...We might be able to give them some guidelines, but we always stay clear as far as we can of grants, because there might be a meeting the night before that you're not aware of that can change their policy.

The normal pattern was to refer clients on, but this was likely to work only where the referral point was both sympathetic and fully informed. Where it was not, the consequences for the client might be very unfortunate. A12, for example, had recently been made redundant, was in his mid-thirties and had two school-age children. He had determined to take up a full-time 'O' level course at the local further education college. A12 visited the Service seeking information on grant aid. He was referred to the appropriate LEA, who subsequently told him that attending the course would attract a grant of £4 per week, but he would forfeit unemployment benefit. The Service itself failed to inform the client that the local college, aware of these restrictions, made concerted efforts to fit adult students into the twenty-one hours per week study limit imposed by DHSS. A12, at one time of follow-up, had given up all ideas of returning to education.

C. *Objective information.* In some respects, the correction of bias in educational information is achieved by comparisons between courses which may be drawn to the attention of the client by the adviser. Such a process presupposes advisers who are themselves adequately informed (and is thus dependent on the Service's information bank) and the willingness of a client to be so informed. At another level, objective information is often dependent on private information, such as judgments on the quality of a particular tutor or the sympathies of an institution. We found that only Service D was prepared to engage in this kind of information provision, and was able to do so not only because of its highly independent status, but also because of its policy of encouraging clients to revisit the Service, when their views on the course or contact to whom they had been referred were solicited. We are not in a position to say whether these clients' opinions, positive or negative, were accurate. Nevertheless, Service D was the only one of the four Services which was able to balance the weight of institutional information with the client's viewpoint. In another way, Services A and B offered some private information, given by advisers from their professional knowledge of an institution or course. Normally, such information was considered to be the province of the linked adviser (as at Service C), but it is unlikely, of course, that such private information will be truly objective. On the other hand we found only small evidence of EGSA advisers presenting a particular institutional bias; and this may be as much ascribed to their more intimate knowledge of particular courses as to an over-zealous loyalty towards the institution. We consider, however, that there is a demonstrable bias towards public sector provision at these four EGSAs, though that bias may be operated in a client-centred way, as at Service D:

> ...What we try to do, very simply...is personalise the system...it's only through doing that that you then give people the opportunity to consider whether it's relevant to their needs or not...

That this approach met with the approval of clients is evidenced by D7's comment that:

> ...Every college has its own idea of how English should be projected and it seems that they're trying to find the right course for...my idea of how I would like to learn my English...

Such a stance has implications for the importance of advisers' intimate grasp of local opportunities and for the employment of sympathetic individuals willing to speak frankly about the quality of particular courses. Again, this approach was most evident at Service D:

> ...I was tapping the private information of the person concerned...she would tell me in fact what was on and what was best in the sense that she would know whether the provision that was down there would be particularly suitable...

D. *Accessible information.* Accessibility, in the sense of physical access, was very different in these four EGSAs from arrangements at a public library. Though all possessed some facilities for browsing, the materials were arranged mainly for the advisers' use, not the clients'. Even so some advisers had considerable difficulty in retrieving information for themselves. This difficulty was noted most at Service B, where advisers were sometimes unfamiliar with the filing systems used. Filing the miscellany of leaflets coming into the office was allocated to the Service's clerical assistant, so that vital information (e.g. details of small educational trusts) was often not brought to the attention of advisers and so was lost to them and to clients. Sometimes advisers had difficulty in retrieving information because of the nature of the source materials. As Service D adviser commented:

> ...I don't want everybody to go around in grey suits, but it would be so nice if all the prospectuses could have some logic behind them.

Services commonly complained of difficulty in locating addresses and telephone numbers; and of the lack of an adequate index.

There were occasions when clients were less than happy to have the adviser so firmly placed between themselves and the Service's information resources. B18's comments illuminate the circumstances in which this might cause problems:

> ...He asked me what I had in mind but really what I wanted was for him not just to suggest things to me but to tell me what there was in City B — what there was available — what sort of classes there were and what sort of things I could become involved with — have lots of leaflets, etc. But really he wanted to know more what I wanted to do.

A number of clients indicated the potential value of a local directory of continuing education provision.

Accessibility of information in the sense of being comprehensible figured far less as a problem for EGSA clients than for library enquirers. Advisers of course had an interpretive role, so in theory at least they could steer clients past the problems of locating the right information and explain what the terms used might mean. Two Services, A and C, had extended this activity to include the production of cross-institution information sheets. At Service C there was evidence that communication of information by telephone is rarely as well comprehended as that confirmed by printed information or conveyed during a personal visit. In at least 25% of cases at this Service, there was firm indication that important items of information had been misunderstood, sometimes to the point where it would inhibit further action. On the other hand, in the case of client C13, who had received a letter confirming verbal information, options had been clearly understood and choices could be made on a more confident basis. There were instances at other Services where clients appeared not to have understood the information provided to them. Advisers appeared largely unaware of the possibility of such mis-apprehensions.

However, clients on the whole expressed broad satisfaction with the information given to them, especially when a range of information was provided and when unexpected additional information was offered. Also much welcomed were named referral contacts prepared to offer personalised assistance. In contrast, D7 commented on his experience of enquiries at individual institutions:

> ...you go to a college...they only hand out information, they haven't really time to talk to you — you just get handed loads and loads of leaflets — don't know what to do with them — write down all these 'phone numbers but no names — and you 'phone up — you don't know who you're talking to...

Most clients accepted what the EGSA had been able to tell them, only a few questioning whether additional information might have been available. Some clients, however, did suspect that there was more to be found out than had been vouchsafed during their EGSA interview. As one client commented on Service B:

> ...I'm sure there must be lots of things going on that I could join or study — I don't know where they are...They seemed to have lots of pamphlets but not very organised. Possibly there was nothing to tell me, not that they couldn't find it.

Clients were likely to express dissatisfaction with the information they received for three reasons. First, they felt that they had not been told anything they didn't already know. Second, they felt that the information was too narrow in range, that the adviser did not have the means to provide the information they sought. As B5 put it:

> ...Well there again she explored every avenue that she knew about.

109

Whether there is other things that she doesn't know about I don't know, so I should say she did as much as she possibly could for me.

Third, in some cases the information could not be relied on to achieve the outcome intended.

As a final and related point, it is important to recognise that clients are not empty vessels to be filled, to whatever level, with new information. They arrive at Services with pre-existing understanding about continuing education's structure and availability. When their own knowledge base is not examined, and where necessary corrected, they may leave the Service with misconceptions intact, which may subsequently prevent full consideration of the new information and thus option take-up. We came across several examples of this factor at work.

Implications

We are very aware that the EGSAs we examined had faced long and difficult struggles to reach the level of information now offered to clients. They were constantly faced with compromises of practice, to meet some at least of the needs presented to them. Sometimes these arrangements had been very successful; and each Service had its own points of excellence. At the same time, clients came to the Service in good faith and in need of thorough and considered assistance. This placed a great responsibility on the advisers; for the information they gave would generally be acted upon by clients.

Services differ in the degree to which they expect clients to pursue information for themselves. While no EGSA can provide every aspect of information on every topic, it seems to us that, since they were initiated to facilitate access, they should do everything they can to ensure the completeness of their own information. This means taking active and on-going steps to fill gaps in their educational information, by lobbying providers and pointing out to them the consequences of failure to supply adequate information in good supply and in good time. These are not new considerations: a recent publication has outlined the kind of information which clients (and therefore EGSAs) may need to know.[35] EGSAs also need to systematise their storage and retrieval systems. This problem is less acute where staff are permanent and full-time, but paramount where staff are temporary and part-time. Urgent consideration needs to be given to ways in which semi-public information may be systematised and shared by all the advisers at a centre, and thus made available, where relevant, to clients. We are in no doubt that access to semi-public information greatly enhances the value of public information, and that Services should make it a matter of policy to obtain such information direct for clients: at least in the areas of admissions requirements, places

110

available and grant aid. Whether or not Services engage in private information is a matter of some delicacy and for the individual Service to resolve. Nevertheless, clients have important experiences which need to be used to alert providers to critical issues, quite apart from their comments on courses. As examples:

(i) they have pertinent views on such matters as Job Centres, the social security system and grants; and
(ii) they have useful comments on the lack of some forms of provision, such as courses on outlying estates.

Clients also have ideas on how EGSAs themselves may be improved. For example, follow-up may demonstrate how adequate was the information provided and thus furnish the Service with a useful guide to its own effectiveness.

These considerations underline the importance of training in information awareness and retrieval skills, both for advisers and for those who have an information-only role, such as clerical assistants. Staff need to be given every opportunity to confirm and extend their own grasp of structure and availability; such competence cannot simply be assumed. They also need training in how their in-house information system operates and in handling complex material, such as the wide range of directories now available in continuing education.

In view of the size of the information task, it is in our view entirely reasonable — as well as diplomatic — that information in vocational guidance is less complete. It cannot be ignored, of course; and cooperative liaison with Job Centres and Careers Advisory Services is essential. Whether or not Services wish to extend their educational information to include the private sector of provision is likely to be resolved by the Service's particular priorities and resources. Again, full coverage is a massive task. For example, the Leeds Educational Information for Adults Project catalogued over 1000 entries for modern language provision in the city alone, when modes of learning such as self-teaching books and private and correspondence courses were taken into account. But in the interests of clients, this is not an area to be ignored; for example, many of the sample identified themselves as engaged in independent learning. There are resources, particularly public libraries, with whom liaison may prove very fruitful.

Some EGSAs may wish to reconsider the ways in which they provide information to clients. We have in mind not only extending browsing facilities, for clients to use privately and uninterrupted, so that they have an opportunity to formulate more clearly the questions they may wish to ask, but also that training is needed in interpreting that information in a way which ensures that clients will understand it. Written confirmation of complex material also appears a little-used practice. Finally, advisers may sometimes need to spend more time on lengthy and thorough information searches for clients, perhaps leading to a follow-up session with the client. More time may also lead to greater accuracy in understanding the clients' own knowledge base and misapprehensions, and pave the way to advice and counselling and implementation. In this way, client-centred as opposed to institution-centred information provision is more likely to be assured.

CHAPTER TEN

ADVICE AND COUNSELLING

Introduction

Advice and counselling are considered jointly in this chapter, since both in discussion and in practice they were often perceived as overlapping by advisers, so that a dividing line was not easily drawn. Clients too faced difficulty in this respect. However, there were some occasions when the distinction between the two functions was clearly perceived by both parties, so some separate discussion is also offered. Thus the chapter considers the Services' approaches to advice and counselling; the amount and type of advice and counselling offered; and some common as well as specific successes and problems. The final section considers the implications of our findings.

Instances of advice and counselling have been drawn from advisers, and clients' accounts of their interviews, in accordance with the definitions given in Chapter 3. It was not always a straightforward task to translate this material into tabulated form; and attention is drawn in the text to areas where such findings should be treated with caution. The same problems sometimes arose with advisers' and clients' ratings of these components of the transaction, and this again is considered in the text.

Approaches to advice and counselling

All four Services taking part in the research perceived advice and/or counselling to be present in some — and usually the majority — of their interviews. Table 20 shows that where advisers were able to identify particular components of guidance as predominant in an interview, advice and counselling were the most predominant after information.

Service A's stated approach to these two functions was the provision of 'basic' advice, with a strong emphasis on referral-on for those clients needing more detailed assistance and, in particular, referral to the Careers Advisory Service, for clients needing counselling. The demand for advice and counselling which had been evidenced to Service A during its first Open Day had come as a surprise:

> ...Thinking back to our first Open Day, very few people spent less than a quarter-of-an-hour talking to somebody and a lot of people spent, you know, half-an-hour — more — even up to an hour in one or two cases — you know, we dealt with 112 people but a lot of that was surprisingly in depth — I think it surprised us — and I think one of the reasons for this is that a lot of people are not sure what they want. I mean, it's fairly straightforward to a person who knows that, you know, he or she wants to do a course in Welding or something like that — you know, say, 'Right —

there's the TOPS course, etc and there's a waiting list' but more often it's a more complex case of somebody who says, 'Well, I've got these qualifications and I think I may lose my job and I'm not quite sure what I'm capable of' — that kind of thing — and that's much more difficult because it's not a question of straight information and it may...well be the case of talking to a person for a while and giving them something and then them coming back a second time. I think it'll be — I would call that somewhere in the middle of advice, you know, rather than in-depth counselling.

Within this framework we have noted variations of approach between individual advisers and in the network of contacts within institutions:

...We were hoping for a sort of definite link person in each institution, and I think we've got it in some cases but we haven't in others...Partly because the institutions themselves don't have a definite link person — I mean, they are departmentally rather than institutionally organised — and I don't think their own admissions process is that good in that respect. Partly, I think also we haven't sort of pushed it hard enough...seem to remember on several occasions we'd tried to get a list together — you know, the named people in each institution — and somehow it never materialised...

Sometimes it was the case that individual institutions were simply uncooperative. As an example, at the local college of further education, the name of the appropriate head of department (information provided anyway in the institution's general information leaflet) was 'the best we could get out of them'. Thus, it was acknowledged that the quality of help offered to the client at the referral point might sometimes be 'very hit-and-miss'.

In all, the personal assistance realistically offered by Service A was seen by us to be quite modest:

...a lot of people will come in with the idea that, you know, they want to go to the OU — they want to go to the FE college — or something — I think this opens their eyes a little bit to the idea that there is a range and maybe they should think about the alternatives before they actually plump for it.

Service B had from its inception been a Service envisaged as offering directly to clients both substantial advice and counselling. Comments from a key informant show this clearly:

...If you take it in theoretical terms, they are three separate things but they overlap — the information, advice and counselling — one can so easily lead to the other. I don't think a Service should give priority to any one of those three — I think it should give the opportunity for the one to lead to the other — to the next one — but if a person comes in and asks for a leaflet on Botany or so-and-so that they shouldn't merely be given the leaflet but they should be given the opportunity to say if they wish to talk about — to discuss it and so on — so I see the counselling element as, if you like — most important would be the wrong phrase to use — but as very necessary. If you're not providing that, you're failing in the sense that there are so many people — or such a high proportion of people — do need the opportunity to discuss their aspirations in the light of their own situation and to be given help in taking the necessary next step.

114

At the same time, with a large advisory team, there were again differences of emphasis between individuals. This informant found it difficult in practice to distinguish between advice and counselling:

> ...I've found it virtually impossible to think of a situation in which you can give advice and not move into a counselling situation really...advice can only be given in relation to what (clients) are and when you get to there, you're into a counselling session.

Other advisers had different views both on how they thought it appropriate to deal with clients and on their approach to referral. This last question caused fundamental problems, as it had for Service A. Despite efforts made to develop named contacts within relevant institutions, the Service felt a degree of insecurity. Such contacts were not intended to contribute such strong advice and counselling as at Service A, but it was anticipated they would provide specialist information and advice, to progress the consideration of choices made during the Service interview. Such contacts were also envisaged as needing to be sympathetic to the aims of the EGSA and the needs of the client. The problems encountered in developing such a network were very similar to Service A's. They were first, the devolved and complex nature of the institutions themselves; second, the difficulties in mounting the intensive outreach necessary to encourage institutions to commit themselves wholeheartedly to cooperation; third, what was characterised as 'institutional rivalry and narrowness' such that:

> ...they may feel threatened by it (the EGSA) and even if they don't feel threatened by it, they may not take the trouble to make the mechanics of the thing work.

Finally, this Service's emphasis on a wide interpretation of education was notable, especially in its attention to the educational opportunities offered by clubs and societies and voluntary organisations.

Service C's approach to advice and counselling was, at least initially, the most devolved of the four EGSAs. Its centre was seen as essential for information-giving and for referral-on when clients were perceived to need advice and counselling. Its network of advisers was to be drawn from 'those already committed to providing advice themselves', although it was anticipated that such contacts would need training in counselling skills. These advisers would deal with clients referred from the centre or from another institution. One Service C centre officer recalled the job description as:

> ...To collect, update, display and disseminate information on educational opportunities in the area...There was never any mention made about what they call counselling work. It was really basically information service.

However, within two years of the formulation of this structure, some major re-orientations were apparent. First, as another centre officer commented:

> ...In practice, what was soon happening was that many enquiries were

made direct to the advisers, who were then passing them on to the office to deal with...

At the same time, the number of linked advisers was growing (it was over eighty at the time of the research); many had little direct involvement with the Service and attempts to introduce training sessions did not arouse interest. Meanwhile, there was some reduction in the contribution offered by those who had given much time initially to get the Service off the ground. In other words, the Service's centre was assuming a larger role than originally envisaged for it. Certainly, some of the closest linked advisers noticed a decrease in the use made of them. It would be wrong to suggest that advice and counselling had become solely EGSA office functions, for they had not. The centre was still information-oriented, as is evidenced in Chapter 9. However, centre staff did perceive themselves to give advice and/or counselling to some of their clients, not only because linked advisers might not be able to do so, but also because these functions were seen to be appropriate in their contact with clients. As one officer suggested:

> ...When people start coming in you realise that you talk to them, and even if you don't think you are counselling, an element of that creeps in just because you are discussing their problems with them and going through things.

There was variation between centre officers in the extent to which they viewed their roles as essentially informational or also advisory/counselling; but all accepted responsibility for identifying clients with such needs.

Service D's positive attitude towards advice and counselling is unequivocally stated in the Service's objectives quoted in Chapter 5. While a network of selected contacts was being established, they were envisaged essentially as detailed information-providers, or, at most, individuals whose advice was reviewed in the light of continued support from the EGSA itself. As one of the Service's staff commented:

> ...I think the initial contact with the person is absolutely essential...because it can affect the whole interaction and it can affect the whole person's life...From personalising it through the first contact we would continue to personalise it as much as possible all the way along the line. I am a great believer in having the person to go along and to have a two-way discussion, because so often I don't think you have a two-way discussion — you have involved application procedures — that isn't a two-way discussion at all...

Service D also had a guarded attitude towards the information-only enquiry, such that the untrained clerical assistant's role was carefully controlled in this respect, in marked contrast with the other Services. For Service D, the information-only response:

> ...presupposes that you've got an informed enquirer in front of you, and very, very often you haven't...

Additionally, and again in contrast with the other Services, Service D considered it essential to be in a position to offer advice on the quality of the courses which might be under consideration for a client:

...the quality of provision is one of the things I'm very interested in looking at, to see exactly what is going on, not what it states is going on...(that) can look fine on paper...

Information gathered from other clients who had had experience of the particular institution or course was given considerable weight, since:

...the consumer's view of what's being offered is in the end the most important view because they are the ones the provision should be there for.

This client-centred advice orientation was offered to those already on courses, as well as to clients considering enrolment, since the structure and approach of some institutions was perceived to be inhibitory for students who had doubts about their courses. Enrolled clients might also find it easier to discuss their future opportunities away from the educational setting in which they were currently placed.

Service D estimated that counselling was offered to around half its clients, while for the rest:

...you're not counselling so formally but you're showing people the stages that they'll be going through once they've decided.

This process of directive counselling might extend to pointing out the degree to which the chosen course might not match the client's aspirations; and it is closely linked to the Service's concern with implementation.

The major constraint which this Service perceived in its advice and counselling activities was that of time, which inhibited not only extended client contact and research on the enquiry, but also outreach work which might develop both the quality and the compass of supportive contacts.

Amount and type of advice and counselling

Table 27 gives the total number of individual options raised, and shows that, overall, clients recalled fewer than advisers. This discrepancy was common to all four Services and to approximately the same degree. Table 28 shows the frequency with which each of the main categories of options was raised (the discrepancy between Tables 27 and 28 in the total numbers of options raised is explained by the fact that within each category a number of specific choices might have been raised, e.g. more than one 'O' level subject). Comparison of Tables 27 and 15 shows clearly the attention paid by advisers to broadening out clients' academic options, and to a lesser extent their leisure and non-vocational options, while vocational courses and career and job options are much less developed. Not all the options raised were subject to discussion in an advisory way.

117

Table 27: EGSA interviews: total number of individual options raised

	Advisers	Clients
Number of options	206	172

Table 28: EGSA interviews: frequency with which each category of option was raised

	Adviser		Client	
Option	Number of instances	Total %	Number of instances	Total %
Leisure	21	13	19	14
Vocational	42	27	29	21
Academic	69	44	58	42
Career and job	26	16	31	23
TOTAL	158	100	137	100

Once again, there were differences between Services. Service B recorded almost twice as many options as Services A and C, which may be accounted for by its generally longer interview time and particular attention to advice and counselling. Service A, it will be recalled, offered 'basic' advice and Service C operated by telephone, largely for information-provision. Service D fell between, perhaps because of its preference for a staged approach. Services B and D (particularly the latter) accounted for most of the discrepancies between advisers, and clients' recall of options. As examples, at Service D, advisers recalled offering seventeen vocational options, clients only six; at Service B, advisers recalled offering thirty-three

Table 29: EGSA interviews: reasons given for option selection

	Adviser		Client	
Reason	Number of instances	Total %	Number of instances	Total %
Same as initial enquiry	50	26	47	38
Personal circumstances	55	28	28	22
Education	28	14	22	18
Work	12	6	6	5
Abilities	16	8	5	4
Potentialities	4	2	3	2
Motivation	8	4	4	3
Aspirations	22	11	10	8
TOTAL	195	100	125	100

academic options, clients only twenty-five. This finding suggests that in a more open advice or counselling setting, clients may find it difficult to grasp fully the alternatives suggested and thus forget or misunderstand them.

This view is supported by Table 29. At Service D, advisers recalled only six instances when options were selected which were the same as the client's initial enquiry; at Service B, there were eleven such instances. The comparison between them and Service C is very clear, with that Service's advisers recalling that all option selections were based on the initial enquiry, and with the fewest discrepancies between adviser and client in the categories of options raised.

Table 29 shows that, as might be anticipated, accordance with the initial enquiry was by no means the only factor taken into account in option selection. It clearly demonstrates the link between assessment and advice (and hence, by implication, information). In comparison with Table 23, it would appear that many of the assessments made of clients were not employed at the point of option recommendation, perhaps because considerations of what provision was actually available for the client loomed large. Nevertheless, the overall message is clear. Advisers often supported their option selection on the basis of assessments which were inconsistently applied and often unshared with clients. The dangers of this approach are evident. Where the option selected is controlled by the adviser, on the basis of misinformed or simply unshared assessments, then the viability of the option may be in doubt. Alternatively, the client may simply discard the option, or fail to understand it. These problems are likely to be exacerbated by failures of the information process; for example, inadequacies in brochures' and prospectuses' information which are not resolved by checking directly with the provider may lead the adviser to fit the client to the provision but in an ill-defined way.

Table 30: EGSA interviews: proportion of interviews where counselling was attempted

Adviser		Client	
Number of interviews	As % of all interviews (n=76)	Number of interviews	As % of all interviews (n=76)
33	43	22	29

Table 30 shows that, according to the advisers, about 4 in 10 interviews involved some counselling; the clients thought about 1 in 3. These figures should be treated with caution, since both advisers and clients were often confused about the two terms, even when aided by considerable explanation. Advisers tended to include such approaches as encouraging the client, or adopting a listening stance, as counselling. Clients sometimes did so too, or simply equated advice-giving with assessment and counselling. In our view, therefore, incidences of counselling were likely to have been fewer than Table 30 show. These matters are considered in more detail later in the chapter.

Conduct of advice and counselling: some problems and successes
Advice and counselling in the interview setting itself again varied considerably between Services.
A. Service A offered directive and non-directive advice to its clients, depending on the style of the particular adviser and whether clients articulated their initial enquiry in a specific and clearly defined way. Advisers tended to be more directive with such clients and to raise fewer options for them. Those with vaguer enquiries were offered a more extensive array. In nearly two-thirds of Service A's cases some recommendation was made to the client, generally in accord with the client's initial enquiry but of a more specific nature. Recommendations were not made when clients had no clearly defined aims at the start of the interview. In these cases, the procedure was to array options before them and to invite consideration outside the interview, with an invitation to return when they felt they were ready for more detailed discussion.

In both circumstances, advisers' discussion of options was unlikely to be highly defined. For example, the possibility of studying for 'O' levels might be pursued, but detailed discussion of particular subjects was unlikely. There were also few concerted attempts to discuss the advantages and limitations of options in great depth, e.g. in terms of finance, location, ability of the client. By and large, clients were presented with the information requested and invited to pursue these matters for themselves. This approach accords with Service A's general purpose of offering 'basic' advice.

However, advisers perceived themselves to have given counselling to thirteen clients; ten clients also thought they had been counselled. Such claims should be treated with caution and not only because it was agreed policy for Service A to refer clients perceived to need counselling to the Careers Advisory Service. Counsellors generally did not differentiate clearly between advice-giving and counselling and some included such functions as reassurance and encouragement under the counselling umbrella. Moreover, only four clients were specifically identified by advisers as being in need of counselling. In these cases, advisers felt their own inadequacy and the frustrations with which clients were faced. As one adviser commented:

> ...The counselling, though...I just don't know if it moved him on at all...we can't always expect to come up with some kind of answer.

B. Service B also offered directive and non-directive advice to its clients, again dependent normally on the attitude of the adviser and the approach of the client. In six cases, where clients knew exactly what they had come for, the preferred option of the client matched the preferred option of the adviser. For the rest, less directive and incomplete advice was offered where clients had a good idea of what they wanted to do, but no immediately suitable option could be discovered. Non-directive advice was usually (but not always) offered to clients with no clear idea what to do; in these cases, as at Service A, a wider array of options was offered.

Discussion of particular options tended to be more detailed than at Service A, and was also more likely to be accompanied by a telephone call to an appropriate institution to check the accuracy of public information, and to discover semi-public information.

Service B advisers perceived themselves to have offered counselling to nine clients; five clients also thought they had been counselled. Once again, there was confusion for some advisers (and clients) in the use of these terms and, interestingly for a Service strongly committed to counselling, quite marked divergences of attitude on the centrality of counselling for clients. One adviser adopted a consciously selective approach:

> ...There was more advising than counselling. He knew what he wanted. I consider that counselling is when you're trying to get somebody's mind...you know, giving them alternatives and saying which could be the best for them and which would perhaps be a little too difficult, I consider that to be counselling. This was merely advising him where he could go. I think you've got to make up your mind which role to play with these people.
> (it's a different role with...)
> ...With different people, yes.

Another adviser had a very strong commitment to counselling and viewed his sessions with clients first and foremost in counselling terms. This adviser felt that he had not done his job properly if he gave information and advice only and if he did not succeed in getting clients to talk in depth about themselves and their circumstances. As an example:

> This man after being made unemployed had gone on the Skillcentre course, which gave him some qualification, and he wanted to supplement that qualification, so I suppose as a result of these two factors, the different atmosphere and the fact that the specific nature of the enquiry as presented did strike me as very plausible, very sensible and of a high degree of urgency in the situation, rightly or wrongly I didn't spend anything like as long as is usual on going back in the person's life history and motivation and so on.

Other advisers' attitudes and practice fell somewhere between these two counselling modes. Pehaps because they were less confident, such advisers appeared to react to the exigencies of the interview rather than to adopt a role.

There was evidence, in the case of Service B, to suggest that directive counselling was used for the purposes described in Chapter 3 with a minority of clients; and a number were invited to revisit the Service for further help. However, counselling might also be used to describe a process of confidence-building and also a vehicle for talking hard facts:

...The big gap was her expecting to get a job — skill equals job — and I had to say skills do not equal job — they just better your chance of getting a job if one comes up for the grabs. That was a very sad thing to do but she took it very well and I got the message across, I think, eventually.

C. The picture at Service C was in many ways clearer than at Services A and B. In line with its self-description as an information centre, enquiries were perceived to be dealt with as articulated by the clients, on the general assumption that clients both knew what they wanted and were capable of assessing their own capabilities. Thus, options were normally dealt with in a non-directive and incomplete way. Directiveness was generally limited to recommendations such as suitability of location, or times at which courses were held, or for vocational or leisure objectives. The question of qualifications did arise; in four cases, clients were told that they were disqualified from certain options on these grounds. For two of these, on the other hand, the adviser was able to suggest alternative routes or methods. While there was divergence of view among advisers about the place of advice at the Service's centre, these differences were in fact little apparent with our sample.

Discussion of the options was again limited, although Service C was very active in checking the accuracy of information and in attempting to obtain semi-public information thought to be relevant.

In marked contrast with Services A, B and D, there was only one instance of substantive counselling. This client was helped first at the EGSA's centre, and then referred on to a linked adviser for more directive assistance.

D. Service D again offered both directive and non-directive advice to its clients, although the former was less in evidence, occurring in just under one-third of cases in the sample. The advisers' preferred approach was an on-going supportive facility wherein the whole range of relevant options might be explored, and indeed one-half of the cases studied at this Service were continuing ones. Typically, during first interviews, options discussed stayed close to the presented enquiry, when this was clearly stated; when it was not, tentative suggestions were made which could be explored in more detail if the client appeared interested. More options were discussed during clients' return visits, when the range of possibilities after contact with tutors and colleges was worked through. Thus, advisers favoured complete and non-directive advice, given over a period of time and supported by assessments and by semi-public and private information, to ensure an adequate match between client and provision.

Service D's insistence that advice should preferably be non-directive arose from a clear concern that clients should reach their own decisions, based on genuine conviction that the goal chosen was appropriate, within a framework of guidance from the advisers and in the light of the clients' own experiences. Advisers emphasised the importance of personalising this process, not only by ensuring wherever possible that clients were referred to named contacts, but also that assessments of clients should match the courses under consideration. Directive advice was used when choices appeared straightforward or when clients were perceived to be approaching decision-making mistakenly.

Service D's discussion of the options raised was generally made in considerable depth and again drew substantially on semi-public and private information. 'Fresh Start' or 'Return-to-Study' courses figured frequently in the option array, largely because they allowed less sophisticated clients the opportunity to explore fields of potential interest.

Service D advisers perceived themselves to have offered counselling to eight clients; four clients accorded with this view. While again advice and counselling were not always clearly distinguished by advisers, interview evidence suggests that some counselling was given. This was sometimes linked with implementation activities. Counselling also included functions such as client reassurance and providing emotional support during clients' periods of self-doubt and anxiety.

In considering the conduct of advice and counselling during the seventy-six cases constituting our sample, our attention was drawn to a number of problems and successes. These are considered in the paragraphs which follow.

A. In line with our view that educational guidance is a cluster, not a linear process, it is very clear that advice is informed by at least two other functions which occur prior to advice-giving or simultaneously with it. The first of these functions is assessment. Assessments are least likely to be applied where a client makes a clearly-articulated enquiry which can be readily matched with an option drawn from the EGSA's information bank. Assessments are most likely to be applied where the client presents a vague or ambiguous enquiry. As we have noted earlier, problems are likely to arise for advice and counselling when assessments are made which are incomplete or unreliable. The second function is information selection, which is likely to be affected by assessment, since advisers will choose or discard options dependent on their view of clients' needs and vice versa; assessments will be dropped in favour of what provision is actually available. This was so even at Service C, when clients were most usually referred to linked advisers or course leaders only after choices from a range of options had taken place. When it comes to advice and counselling, a great deal depends on the adequacy of the information bank and the adviser's skill in manipulating it.

B. The particular strengths and weaknesses of these EGSAs' information resources have been examined in Chapter 9, but some confirmatory points may be made here. First, there was a clear and general preference, in the range of options selected for clients, for courses in the local public institutions and a tendency to consider the more traditional forms of provision. Perhaps this reflected the advisers's limited confidence in the information area or the particular emphasis of the Service's information bank. Some clients who expected a wide range of options expressed disappointment with this approach and tended to lose confidence in the adviser:

> ...all she seemed to suggest was I went to a college...and did a...course in 'A' levels...I wouldn't mind...if I thought it was of any practical value to me...I've got an ONC...which I was told was a sort of equivalent...so I said...wouldn't I be just backtracking...she didn't really seem to know. (A9)

Second, the adviser's biases, unconscious or otherwise, already noted in Chapter 8, would continue to operate at the advice stage. Thus, at Service C for example, there was evidence that men and women were likely to be channelled into quite different vocational directions. Men were directed towards computing courses (C17 and C18), while women's opportunities included education (C1, C5 and C11), social work (C3 and C7), art and design (C4), catering (C6, C12 and C15), secretarial skills (C9, C10 and C13), beauty and floristry (C14). Two women clients at this Service spontaneously indicated to the research fieldworker that they felt certain assumptions had been made about them because they were female. As an example, the case of C16 involved a husband and wife enquiry about a leisure opportunity to study an Amateur Radio course. Although it was the wife who finally took details of the course, she remarked on the impression she formed over the telephone that the EGSA adviser was disappointed not to be able to discuss the option with her husband. The office record in this case confirms that an assumption was made that it was the husband's and not a shared interest.

Third, and again as evident in Chapter 9, the information provided was not always sufficiently accurate or detailed to reveal the practical difficulties for a particular client.

C. The way in which matters raised in (A) and (B) above may jointly produce an unfortunate outcome for the client is vividly illustrated in the case of client A13. On the surface, A13's was an apparently straightforward interview with few problems. The client, whose children were growing up, was keen to get back to work and to widen her opportunities by gaining 'O' level qualifications. The adviser made a fairly detailed assessment of A13's personality, educational and work background and family circumstances, and provided her with the relevant leaflets detailing available 'O' level courses, confident that she could pursue the information given and make a return visit if any problems arose. In view of the limited financial resources available to A13, adviser and client came to the conclusion that a part-time course would be most suitable. However, after independently pursuing the possibility of grants, the client was told that a full-time course would attract a small grant to cover books and course fees and, having come to the conclusion that these could not otherwise be afforded, she plumped for the full-time course. Full-time courses at this particular college of further education demanded that aspiring students sit an entrance examination. This information was given in the college pamphlet but no details were available on the level of difficulty. A13 telephoned the EGSA office, who referred her to the college itself for more detailed information. She was told no preparation was necessary, as the test was merely devised to assess general ability. She was both horrified and distressed to discover, on arriving to sit the examination, that she was required to answer questions in geometry and algebra, with which she had had no dealings for over fifteen years. As a result, A13 failed the examination and was refused admission to the course. More careful consideration of assessment, full information and detailed advice might have prevented a very distressing situation for the client. This case also illustrates the need for advisers to appreciate the often long experiential gap in clients' understanding of educational procedures. It is all too easy for advisers familiar with these procedures to overlook how daunting and confusing they can be for the educationally inexperienced. Thus, implementation is implicit also within the assessment, information, advice and counselling functions.

In contrast, an example of how an EGSA may avert a negative outcome for a client by attending closely to such matters is provided by one of Service D's sample. Client D10's initial enquiry related to a request for help in filling out a lengthy and complex Open University application form. The details of the form provided the vehicle for assessment, in the light of which the adviser recommended to D10 that she enrol for a 'Fresh Start' course, on the grounds that it would enable her to develop necessary study skills:

...I felt that if she was going to be serious about doing an OU course, and had not really done any systematic studying since — it would be a nicer way to try and get back into it. If she is going to have to write essays for the OU, she is going to have to learn...to write essays anyway, and also, being on an OU course she is not going to have a tutor close to her, whereas (tutor X) will always be there. Even if she does the course...for just one term, I am sure he will give her the backing for the OU if she needs it — she can always go back to him, and discuss things, and books that she has read and worked on. I think it would be good for her to meet a lot of other new people as well, and that course looks as though it's got a really good age-group.

At follow-up, D10 was found to have abandoned the Open University course, finding it 'too heavy-going', but was pursuing the 'Fresh Start' course with enthusiasm.

D. Clients who appeared articulate and confident or for whom a ready answer could apparently be supplied were not always best served by such a direct approach. We have noted elsewhere that at Service C the telephone produced its own inhibitions. So client C6, who made an enquiry about catering, was given information about two local courses. When further investigation on her own part revealed that she was unlikely to get a grant, she was about to give up when her husband independently got information about an appropriate TOPS course from the Job Centre. It emerged in interview that C6's optimum goal was to establish her own business, but this had not been exposed in the initial enquiry, so she had received no advice about support for small businesses or about courses on how to set up in business. It would be misleading to overstate such cases, since others were resolved by a 'face-value' response, but this problem was experienced by some clients at all four EGSAs. Some clients responded to the 'What can I do for you?' opening remark by making suggestions which were no more than mere possibilities, but these suggestions were often taken as considered aims and other options were not raised. Clients tended to attribute this outcome to their own behaviour. One Service A client recalled, 'I didn't get much out of it — perhaps I stressed this language aspect too much and I think perhaps channelled him in one direction'. The researcher's interview with the adviser concerned indicated that great pains had been taken to come up with something which would fit this client's 'strong desire to use his languages'. The message is clearly that EGSAs should be wary of clients' stated aims and probe clients as to how serious these are before concentrating exclusively on them. We also consider that particular attention should be paid to the 'leisure' client in this respect. Usually our EGSAs subscribed to the view that 'people looking for leisure courses usually know what they are looking for, and just want to know where to find it'; yet the clients in this sample with leisure enquiries almost always had an additional vocational intent. This finding accords with our studies of library enquirers.

E. The problem of identifying just what the client's advice needs are extended clearly into the counselling function. Except at Service C, where very little counselling was offered, clients were consistently less likely to recognise themselves as having been counselled than were advisers to recognise they had given counselling. It is difficult to envisage how the term counselling may be applied to a process where one party is unaware of it; on the other hand, this may be explained by the advisers' tendency to ascribe listening and encouragement stances to this function. There were several clients who felt they would have benefited from counselling and who felt they had been unable to get this point across in interview:

126

It's a bit difficult, because as I say, he gave me good advice but it's not exactly what I wanted to hear — not to hear but I wanted more advice in the general sense. I mean, he gave me advice on what to do from what I've got, but not, 'Is it really what you want, are you in the right job, can I help you in that way?' He didn't ask me to talk about myself or anything. (B2)

D15 certainly came to the EGSA in need of counselling (as well as of assessment):

...I need to talk to somebody about it and make them decide from what I've got — qualifications, and what I'm interested in — whether they think that I'm able to cope, whether I am motivated actually.

This client failed to understand Service D's staged approach to advice and counselling and so blamed herself for overattention to the first enquiry:

...It's not just that course actually, but I think when I mentioned that I was a nurse he homed in on that...which isn't exactly what I wanted to do, but I didn't actually bother to tell him, so it's probably both people being a little bit unsure of what the other person was thinking...I wasn't asking probably the right questions. I'd like to have asked more but I didn't quite know how to go about it...so though I found it helpful, I still feel that I'm on my own, as it were, whereas I think what I was looking for was more counselling, more guidance, because I feel like a fish out of water...

In contrast, the adviser concerned perceived the interview as:

...an initial enquiry regarding a specific piece of information...the first contact in what I imagine will be a continued contact...I feel she has come in, is looking at a long-term prospect — she doesn't need anything at the moment...

There were almost no reported instances where clients specifically asked for counselling by name.

At Service C, where the telephone was found to present problems in terms of the conveying of information and advice, it was clearly seen by clients and advisers alike to be impossible in such a delicate area as counselling. Counselling need remained almost unrecognised; however, in the estimation of the research worker, no less than fourteen of the clients she herself interviewed in Service C's sample indicated a need for counselling. Failure to identify such a need could have had serious implications for the client. C2 provides an illustration of these points. This client posed a question about First Aid courses, was judged to be seeking straightforward information and was given two telephone numbers of providers to contact. In her interview with us she explained:

...I want something to do, you see. I've got no hobbies apart from the usual knitting and reading...I feel as if I have no outside interest apart from the home and the kids — I feel I'm at the stage where I could do with something to fill a couple of evenings in, you know, and that's really all I am cut out to do.

Later she revealed that daytime was more problematic and that she would like to find out about wider options that might suit her interests, but:

...I didn't like to ring up and say, 'I'm looking for something to do in the evenings — or the afternoons. Could you...?' I thought that that would be a bit much to ask people, you know, over the telephone to say, 'I'm interested in taking up a hobby'.

C2 also explained that First Aid arose merely as something she already had a little confidence in, as she worked part-time as an auxiliary nurse, but her main difficulties lay in loneliness within her community and a feeling of waste in having left school with no qualifications. She mused over the possibility of voluntary involvement in family support schemes which might ease her loneliness and give her a sense of purpose, but wondered if she'd be more of a nuisance.

There were occasions when Service C centre advisers gauged there might be more to an enquiry, but did not act on this instinct. As an example, C14 wanted to study a beautician's course, was told she was not qualified, and was offered a course in floristry instead, which she rejected. The adviser reflected in interview, 'I think in this case really, when you go back to the beginning, after all the information you have got, that (C14) was certainly in need of counselling'.

Service C was not of course the only Service which faced difficulties in identifying and pursuing counselling need, but it was most evident here. On the other hand, it was also possible to over-engage in this function, by pursuing a counselling path which the client considered inappropriate. A Service B adviser provided an illustration of this point, commenting on a particular client thus:

...She was very vague. The only thing she mentioned early on was philosophy, and she didn't seem to know really what she meant by philosophy, but it came out after a long time that she was friendly with somebody...who taught in the Philosophy of Education, and she'd obviously talked about this with him and found it interesting...later on in the interview it transpired that she was about to have been married, a doctor I think, and emigrate to Greece, and although she didn't say very much about this, I felt that this experience — the failure of this experience, if you like — was fairly traumatic and was causing her to question the whole of her future life and her present position and so on...

The client, however, said:

...I wanted to study something because I was bored, but I wasn't sure what was available...He was very nice and helpful but didn't really tell me anything...I don't think I needed counselling as such — just information...

F. Part of the problem lies in the fact that clients are not always clear what is available from the Service, or what they may legitimately expect from it, quite apart from confusions over terms such as counselling. To this may be added a more generalised unease about presenting themselves for assistance in the first place. As C7 put it:

...I think people tend to think that educational and careers advice stops at eighteen; probably a lot of people don't think they can get advice after that and maybe feel very awkward about coming forward and asking for it.

Implications

Before discussing specific implications for the development of practice, we consider it important to point out just how difficult many advisers felt it was to provide adequate advice and counselling to their clients. Quite apart from the fact that two Services depended almost entirely on voluntary support to continue, these tasks are enormously complex and have made great demands on the staff concerned. It is a measure of many advisers' concern that they have maintained such a commitment, even when aware of the limitations of such help as they could provide. The personal toll that advice and counselling work may take was described by one Service D adviser thus:

> ...For people for whom you are explaining why (the system) doesn't work for them, it's an incredible emotional drain — you tend to forget about the people whom you do advise...and you do get on to something that they want...Those, if you like, are successes...ten successes don't outweigh the one unsuccessful person for whom you just have to say, 'I'm sorry, I can't see anything that we can offer for you'.

By and large, Services were engaged in directive and incomplete advice for those clients who appeared to know what they wanted to do, and incomplete and non-directive advice for those who did not. There was no evidence to suggest that one form of advice-giving, when used appropriately, was superior to another — except that all Services experienced problems in identifying clients who appeared to be confident in their intents, but who in interview with us were not so. This meant that many clients in need of wider advice or of counselling did not avail themselves of these opportunities; it clearly indicates that advisers and indeed all workers at an EGSA need careful awareness and diagnostic training. Even where advice and counselling were used, there were problems in the assessment and information functions which might act to invalidate the help offered. Sometimes, it appeared to us that the advice and counselling given, sound in its own terms, failed to be accepted by clients because they could not identify with it or perhaps understand fully the options presented. All this argues for more time to be spent with clients during interview, sharing the assessment, information and advice process, perhaps with information in written form to enable clients to consider the options proposed. Another strategy may be to encourage clients much more strongly to revisit the EGSA. They very rarely did so at Services A, B and C, although, as we have noted earlier, this was quite common practice at Service D. Some Services, staffed by a volunteer team, will face problems of ensuring continuity with such a strategy; those enjoying full-time staffing will not. We suspect that ease of location may also be critical; while clients may make a 'special effort' once, they might not be prepared to do so over a number of visits. In such cases, the importance of a thorough and consistent follow-up is underlined:

it may be advisable to engage the client's interest in communicating by telephone or by letter.

A follow-up strategy may also bring benefit to the EGSA, through an opportunity to test out how complete and reliable their advice has been. This raises the question of the role of network contacts or links. It is clear that EGSAs do not always enjoy enthusiastic and comprehensive cooperation in this matter, and even where they do, the contribution that such individuals may realistically make is open to question. When they are untrained and/or appointed on a hierarchical basis, there is no reason to assume that contacts are automatically competent to provide advice and counselling in the way that is most helpful to clients. Even where these contacts are intended to provide a source for information only, it may be very difficult for them not to adopt an advisory role. These matters point to the importance of training for contacts. It may be that institutions will become more enthusiastic if they are kept regularly informed of the numbers and types of clients sent to them, are included in Services' outreach programmes, and are regularly updated on the difficulties — and successes — that clients have faced.

For EGSAs, this institutional outreach implies thorough record-keeping and consistent follow-up. It also means they must be sure they have accurately gauged their clients' main needs and they record how far it was truly possible to match the client with available provision. This is sometimes at odds with a very human desire to find *something* to resolve the enquiry. Services were aware that 'numbers referred' was an important tool in convincing institutions of the importance of the EGSA's work. We also heard evidence that institutions sometimes doubted whether they had in fact benefited from the referrals recorded. This suggests either that drop-out is high, or that contacts did not know the source from whom the client was referred. In either case, EGSAs should take note.

We noted a general bias towards public sector provision, and some personal biases among advisers. Also apparent was variability of attitude and emphasis between advisers within an EGSA. This meant that the assistance received was to some extent dependent on the approach of the adviser encountered. Services also had a particular style, dependent on their policy, structure and funding, which generally dictated their construct of the client, in particular how far clients could resolve their enquiries unaided. Two points may be made here. The first is that it appears to us that inconsistency of approach *within* Services is undesirable and also avoidable, given thorough attention to training and to procedures for self-monitoring. The second is that inconsistency *between* Services is currently unavoidable, given the fact that many exist only because of the most ingenious manipulation of the woefully inadequate funding available to them. Moreover, standardisation is unwise, since different settings and objectives require different strategies. However, we consider that whatever the particular structure and approach devised, Services need to face the fact that their own aims may be modest, but their clients' needs will not be.

Many clients appeared unsure about what they might expect from the EGSA and how they should proceed while there. This difficulty increased advisers' problems in identifying clients who might need more help than the enquiry itself appeared to suggest. EGSAs may need to consider ways in which they can educate their users in how to use the Service, a matter which has implications for how EGSAs advertise themselves. Advisers need to have the skills to manipulate an interview so that clients are enabled to reveal what their hopes and expectations are. This is particularly the case with counselling, where clients appeared often very unsure of the meaning of the term and hence of its relevance to them.

CHAPTER ELEVEN
REFERRAL AND IMPLEMENTATION

Introduction
Referral and implementation are considered together in this chapter, since they were often linked in practice. Usually this was because advisers considered referral to be part of implementation, though in our view the latter function has a quite distinct identity.

This chapter examines Services' approach towards referral and implementation; the amount and type of referral and implementation; the conduct of referral and implementation as it arose at the four Services; and some implications for practice.

Approaches to referral and implementation
In our view, referral may be an information-based or an advice/counselling-based activity, dependent on the policy of the Service (and of individual advisers); the perceived needs of clients; and the particular enquiry. Services' policies on referral may thus be gathered from the descriptive accounts given in Chapter 5, their approaches to information (Chapter 9) and their policy on counselling (Chapter 10). In summary, Service A's policy on referral was clear from its self-description as a basic information and advice Service. Referral to institutions in the locality was envisaged as essential for fuller information and advice. Service B shared something of this view, though it saw itself as providing more information and adopted a more fundamental attitude towards advice and counselling. Service C was in theory purely an information service, with assisted referral to a network of linked advisers to offer more information as well as general advice and counselling — though we noted that this role was changing. Service D saw itself as providing all the guidance facilities to its clients, with referrals made in the light of on-going support for those referred, should they need it. These referrals were made primarily for information purposes. Thus, in policy terms, Services differed in the amount of help they gave clients directly and in their views of what referral was to do. Differences of practice by advisers within a Service added to this variety of practice.

All Services experienced problems with their referral networks. These were recognised to be difficult and time-consuming to establish in such a way that the contact was competent to meet the demands made by clients and also sympathetic to the aims of the Service. Services often found themselves unable to persuade an institution to nominate the right individual contact, or indeed any contact at all. At the time of the research, no Service had succeeded in systematising its recruitment and organisation of these necessary links to its own satisfaction; Service C perhaps came nearest. No Service had been able to provide training for them. Coverage was often dependent on the Services' ability to recruit sympathetic individuals in a piecemeal way. Services also varied in the degree to which they had made effective outreach to Job Centres, voluntary agencies and other relevant bodies.

Chapter 5 also considers the Services' differing policies towards implementation. For Service A this function was undeveloped, though it was a matter under discussion at working party level. Service B generally favoured implementation, but practice was at the discretion of individual advisers. Examples of advocacy were offered to us; coping assistance did not figure notably; and feedback was limited and unsystematic. Service C had identified in an early statement a need to identify 'enquiries which call for educational provision not currently available', which may be taken to imply both an advocacy and a feedback function. We were offered examples of client advocacy which had been undertaken as the occasion presented. Feedback was characterised as much like Service B's:

> ...we do sometimes make noises to education authorities but nobody ever actually gets figures and presents anything official.

although instances of the Service's success in encouraging new courses were also provided. Service D had no doubts about the importance of implementation. This approach perhaps reflects its strong connections with the adult literacy movement and may account for its commitment to providing coping assistance to its clients. As examples, assistance in filling out application forms was commonly given and was sometimes used for providing other functions of educational guidance. As one of our informants at this Service commented, '...counselling — and the enabling — in my mind come together'. Clients might also be given direct assistance in preparing for their intended course:

> ...he can't start until (September) so why not try and point him in the right direction where he can read a couple of books — he can get back into studying — We're often pointing out, 'It's not the fact you don't have the ability — you just haven't had the opportunity to develop that ability — don't try and do too much too soon'.

This Service also placed a strong emphasis on advocacy: sometimes successful, sometimes not. It clearly felt a great concern for those it described as 'the walking wounded', for whom no suitable provision could be found, and saw it as an essential role to press for resource reallocation on such clients' behalf. So Service D was actively engaged in feedback. Its major inhibitor was perceived to be inadequate funding, which caused matters such as systematised follow-up to be given a lower priority than more immediately pressing matters. We have earlier noted that this Service, perhaps because of its informality and easy accessibility, was much more successful in having clients return to it for further consultation. This meant that the Service had an in-built client follow-up mechanism, albeit partial, and clients who did return provided additional data which might be utilised in feedback.

Amount and type of referral and implementation

Table 31 shows the further actions to be taken by advisers and clients, according to the perceptions of each. Advisers recorded providing rather less in the way of referral and implementation than they recommended clients to do for themselves; this was the case, in broadly the same degree, for all Services. Clients recorded fewer instances of the adviser acting, or intending to act, on their behalf, and saw themselves as having to do more than the advisers recalled. Clients reported having to do least for themselves at Service C (58% of all client-perceived instances of further actions) and most at Service A (78%). Thus referral and implementation at all four Services were shared activities, with the balance of responsibility on the client.

Table 31: EGSA interviews: further actions

	Adviser perceived		Client perceived	
Action to be taken by	Number of instances	Total %	Number of instances	Total %
Adviser	51	40	42	34
Client	77	60	80	66
TOTAL	128	100	122	100

Table 32: EGSA interviews: analysis of adviser actions

	Adviser perceived		Client perceived	
Action	Number of instances	Total %	Number of instances	Total %
Telephone call	39	77	31	74
Letters/notes	12	23	11	26
TOTAL	51	100	42	100

Table 32 shows that the advisers' referral and implementation activities consisted of telephone calls in three-quarters of cases. Many of these calls were made for the purposes of checking information for later relaying to the client; others were to check on such matters as enrolment procedure. These may broadly be encompassed within referral, since they were essentially referral activities conducted on the client's behalf. Services B and C accounted for over 70% of these instances between them; Service A only one. Over one-third of the instances of written communication are accounted for by Service A, which left notes for personnel at the Careers Advisory Service in which it was housed. Only about one-third of advisers' actions were directly concerned with implementation and the majority of these were conducted by Service D. Usually these were to effect introductions or appointments for clients, which comes within the compass of coping activities. Occasionally there was some advocacy, when alternative entry requirements were discussed. (The discrepancy between advisers' and clients' perceptions shown in this Table is accounted for by the fact that actions were sometimes conducted out of interview and not always declared to the client).

Table 33: EGSA interviews: analysis of client actions

Action	Adviser perceived		Client perceived	
	Number of instances	Total %	Number of instances	Total %
Telephone call	22	27	28	35
Letter	12	16	14	18
Personal call	27	35	21	26
Contact unspecified	16	21	17	21
TOTAL	77	100	80	100

Table 33 shows that actions recommended for clients took a different pattern. According to the advisers, about one-third of clients' actions were to be personal calls at a specific institution; and about one in five were more generalised actions. These client-recommended actions took the form mostly of self-referral for further information and advice. Table 33 also shows some confusion between clients' and advisers' understandings of whether the call recommended should be by personal visit or by telephone.

The overall picture shows advisers doing what they can, by checking details to help clients on their way, by direct or indirect referral and occasionally by implementation. The onus of further actions lies with clients themselves; indeed, they perceived themselves to have a greater share of the responsibility than did the advisers. Within this broad picture, the nature of what clients were expected to do for themselves depended on the stance of the Service.

Conduct of referral and implementation: some problems and successes
Advisers were generally confident that clients were competent to pursue the further actions recommended to them, though the cut-off point varied between Services and between individual advisers. As a Service B adviser commented:

...Perhaps I am out on a limb here as far as (advisers) are concerned but that is partly due to the numbers that are involved. I feel that she was perfectly capable of, and it's essential if she is going to achieve what she's out to achieve, that she will have to take initiatives herself, so I didn't feel that it would be any real help to her for me to do the very elementary spadework which is necessary for her to pursue the lines I have suggested. But other (advisers) would feel differently.

In contrast, Service D's policy, applied generally to clients, was expressed as:

...If only we can leapfrog over the general office enquiry...it's going to be difficult to get to see who you want to see which is why we tend to do that implementation side of it.

Sometimes, practical constraints were influential. Reflecting on why clients were asked to take the responsibility themselves, a Service C adviser explained that it:

...would save the to-ing and fro-ing between the office and client...It's not a question of passing the buck.

And advisers at Services A and B felt the constraints of interviewing when institutions were shut. Since these advisers worked on a rota of occasional attendance, pursuing an enquiry the next day was rarely considered to come within the role expected of them.

However, there is no doubt that clients who were offered assisted referral and/or implementation were very appreciative of this assistance. At Service C, for example, there were clients for whom specific appointments had been made, or whose name had been given to linked advisers who would contact them. Such actions appeared to provide encouragement to those clients who lacked the courage to take the first steps. Thus B19 commented:

...Downstairs in the Job Centre they weren't very helpful really. But he seems to have put me in touch with the people who I need to see, you know, seems to have broken down what I usually look on as red tape.

and C4 appreciated the extra actions taken on her behalf in the way of telephone calls;

...He was really helpful. He rang back about three or four times, I mean he did everything he could.

but when it came to being advised to take her own action, she explained,

...Actually, he told me to go to the Careers Centre and told me which name to get and he gave me a lot of names, but I never really went to the Careers Centre because I haven't much faith in the Careers Centre...I don't really like going.

Those clients who had pursued unassisted referrals for information and advice had sometimes found that the referral turned out to be inappropriate, because the course was full, or unsuitable. A11 provides an example. He was adjudged to need no help in pursuing his agreed goal and was provided with unassisted referral information typical of this Service's approach. In following the actions recommended to him, he found first that the course was full and second, that there was another, alternative course which he thought would be more suitable for him. However, as college staff did not inform him in detail of the demands of the entrance examination (which he considered he could easily have met had he known them), he was refused admission. By the time their decision was communicated to him, it was already too late for him to pursue the original, recommended goal.

It was also (though exceptionally) the case that advisers could be too assiduous. By pressing clients into lines of action not fully in accord with their own understanding, some clients found themselves propelled into courses which they later rejected. A client at Service B found herself in this position. She had been assessed as 'very hesitant' and given all the referral assistance the adviser could provide. This client was discovered at follow-up to have been accepted on a course, but had never attended. She had since found work, which she said in interview had been her prime reason for approaching the Service in the first place.

There were examples of activity within our sample which fell squarely into the category of implementation. Nearly all were concerned with fairly modest acts of advocacy. At Service B, an adviser successfully used personal contacts to have clients admitted to courses (in one case where the client was not formally eligible). Service C showed a willingness to negotiate entry into an ongoing course, where qualifications were not an important prerequisite: successfully in the cases of clients C8 and C9 and unsuccessfully in the case of C16. There seemed more reluctance to assume a role of advocacy for clients who could not reach formal matriculation requirements for a vocational course. Clients C4 and C14 were recommended to follow courses to obtain the requisite qualifications, before seeking entry to the courses of their choice — though client C6 was instructed that if she could obtain an interview herself she might be accepted on performance rather than on formal requirements.

At Service D there were numerous instances of helping the coping activity of clients. D2 was thought likely to run into 'red-tape' problems, in pursuit of his goal of enrolling for a car mechanics course:

...In this instance...the automatic response from the department was, 'No, it's not appropriate until such-and-such a time', and it was only because I was in a position to explain the background to circumstances, that they were then in a position to make a decision as to whether or not it would be appropriate for him to see somebody. And I think had he done that, he may well have got slightly shorter changed than he was entitled to, which was why I did the implementing in that instance. He is now in the position to implement the rest himself, because he has got somebody to go along and see.

It should be noted that D2 was an on-going client, considered to be now sufficiently prepared to cope alone.

137

Implications

From our evidence it appears that clients found assisted referral, based on complete information (especially of the semi-public kind), very encouraging; and acts of advocacy were especially appreciated. It is apparent that, once again, educational guidance must be viewed as a cluster, not a linear process. As an example, the impact of advisers' assessment on their judgment of clients' competence in implementation was important. However, we note that whether or not clients received these forms of assistance might depend on factors unrelated to their actual or perceived need. It would be unrealistic and sometimes inappropriate to offer all clients such help as assisted referral. Some were quite happy to pursue matters for themselves; in other cases these activities may place too much pressure on the client. However, in general, clients were very well disposed to actions of this kind and made use of them. A point which emerges clearly is that it is not always possible for advisers to discern which clients will need help most, either because of inadequate assessment or because advisers' own awareness of the difficulties clients face at the end of the referral chain is limited. This latter problem may be exacerbated by advisors' lack of enagagement with institutions directly. In this way, the inadequacies in their information and hence advice base may remain unrevealed to them.

We were very aware of the problems Services faced in ensuring a network of contacts which was both complete and appropriate, with implacable indifference sometimes very evident.

Nevertheless, the importance of outreach to encourage such institutions to change their views is clear; where institutions were co-operative, the links made were appreciated by advisers and clients.

We consider that referral and implementation activity, systematically and sensitively conducted, is additionally important in bringing Services up against the realities experienced by clients and is a healthy antidote to any complacency. In that connection, client follow-up is central to advocacy and particularly to feedback. It is hard to see how Services can meet all clients' advocacy needs if they are not followed up, and even harder to see how feedback may be fully representative of clients' needs without these essential data. Service D maintained what might be termed a self-generated follow-up, dependent on clients' returning for further assistance. This approach was inherently self-selective and non-systematised, but it was the only widespread follow-up in operation at any of the four EGSAs. Service C was tackling feedback in a different way, albeit to a limited degree. This Service was systematically collecting evidence of unmet demand for word-processing courses locally. Client C13 was just one of the large number of clients enquiring for this subject to go on a waiting list compiled by the Service and taken directly to the linked adviser of the college most likely to meet the demand.

138

CHAPTER TWELVE
THE RATINGS SCALES

Introduction

To obtain a measure of the level of satisfaction with the main functions of the client/adviser interviews (assessment, information, advice and counselling), together with perceived overall value, both clients and advisers were asked to rate the value of these aspects on a scale of 0 to 10. Mean ratings were then calculated for each of the five aspects from the viewpoint of clients and of advisers. Individual ratings for each factor were included only where both parties had made a judgment. Normally, this meant that each mean represented the central tendency of all but one or two of the sample. However, in the aspect of counselling, where clients *and* advisers generally considered counselling not to have been a component of the interview, the means are based on only a few cases. These five pairs of means formed a basis first, for evaluating advisers' and clients' own levels of satisfaction with components of the interview and second, for comparing satisfaction levels as between the two parties.

It should be noted that these ratings scales were administered soon after the EGSA interview, and thus in all cases before clients' final outcomes had been determined. For this reason, implementation activity was not included in the functions rated. Clients and advisers were, however, asked to offer a prognosis of outcome; this is considered in Chapter 13.

Assessment

Table 34: Rating of guidance functions: assessment, clients' and advisers' ratings (means)

Service	Client	Adviser
D	8.4	5.5
A	5.4	7.0
B	6.0	7.7
C	7.2	8.6

Table 34 compares the ratings made by clients and advisers of the assessment component of the interviews at the four EGSAs. It is immediately apparent that in Services A, B and C, clients were less satisfied with the assessment they understood to have been made of them than were the advisers. Clients were least satisfied at Services A and B, where, it will be recalled, they had limited awareness of the assessment process enacted by advisers. Assessments were rated higher by Service C clients, although these assessments were generally of a restricted, often concrete or factual nature, as might be expected in telephone interactions. Conversely, advisers at Services A, B and C consistently rated their assessments more highly than clients and to approximately the same degree. The result at Service D is discrepant, with advisers rating their satisfaction with their assessment of clients much lower than did the clients themselves. In our view, this is attributable to these advisers' cautiousness with assessment, which, in line with the Service's overall approach, was a staged procedure. Service D advisers were also very aware of the deficiencies in their own powers of assessment, particularly in the area of potentiality. Clients at this EGSA, however, favoured the open and informal approach adopted at the Service, as D7's comments illustrate:

...he's ever so easy to talk to...easy, informal, relaxed...relaxed — that's the main thing really.

Information

Table 35: Rating of guidance functions: information, clients' and advisers' ratings (means)

Service	Client	Adviser
D	8.1	7.2
A	5.9	8.0
B	7.7	7.8
C	8.2	9.6

Table 35 compares the ratings made by clients and advisers of the information component of the interviews at the four Services. Clients at all Services rated this function more highly than assessment, with the greatest difference apparent in clients' ratings for Service B, which was seen to offer a particularly wide range of information provision. However, clients' ratings were highest for Services C and D's provision, with clients at C especially appreciative of the rapid conveyance of up-to-date information and at D of semi-public and private information. Service A's provision of 'basic' information was lowest-rated. Again, advisers at A, B and C rated this function more highly than clients, and at all four EGSAs, more highly than the assessment function. At Service C, advisers were clearly very confident of the value of their information provision. The largest discrepancy between advisers' and clients values was at A, with advisers much more confident than clients that the information provided was satisfactory. There was again a discrepant result at D, where advisers rated the information component lower than did clients themselves, attributable, we think, to these advisers' clear understanding of the insecure nature of educational information and of the existence of information which was not yet provided to clients.

Advice and counselling

Table 36: Rating of guidance functions: advice, clients' and advisers' ratings (means)

Service	Client	Adviser
D	8.3	6.4
A	6.4	7.1
B	6.1	7.5
C	7.8	8.9

Table 36 compares the ratings made by clients and advisers of the advice component of the interviews at the four Services. Clients at most Services rated this function of educational guidance higher than assessment, but at Services B and C gave it a lower rating than information, while at Services A and D it was given a higher value. A number of Service-specific reasons for these results may be offered. At Service C clients tended to perceive advice as an extension of information and so the result here reflected the high rating given for information; the same is true for advisers. At Service B, clients' means were adversely affected by consistently low ratings given for one adviser, whose approach to advice was highly directive, irrespective of the clients' approach. We consider that the ratings offered by clients for Services A and D are a more consistent reflection of clients' satisfaction with the advice function. Again, it is clear that Service A's 'basic' approach is less valued than the staged, supportive and shared approach of Service D, although clients did perceive themselves happier with advice provided by Service A than with its assessment and information provision. Advisers' results at Services A, B and C again showed a consistent over-rating of the advice function when compared with clients, which was strongest at Service B, though this was also subject to the particular distortion considered earlier in this paragraph. The discrepant result at Service D is also in evidence with advice.

Table 37: Rating of guidance functions: counselling, clients' and advisers' ratings (means)

Service	Client	Adviser
D	7.1	5.0
A	5.8	5.2
B	4.5	6.8
C	0.3	4.7

Table 37 compares the ratings made by clients and advisers of the counselling component of the interviews at the four Services. We have noted earlier that both clients and advisers expressed some confusion between this function and advice. In our view, much of what both parties termed as counselling fell into the advice category, so although advice ratings may be treated with confidence, these counselling ratings are less secure. They are also based on fewer cases, for in many instances no rating was offered, since counselling was not considered by either party to have arisen. This was particularly the case at Service C, where the means represent an 'n' of only three. Additionally, ratings have been excluded where only one party to the transaction made a response. These factors weaken any inferences which may be drawn, so those that follow are offered tentatively.

It does appear that counselling was rated lowest of the interview functions by clients, which may be attributable to its more abstract conceptual basis. Clients were not clear what they might expect of this function and some hoped that it might move them on more than the process offered appeared to do. Thus A1's comment that:

> ...It makes a change to talk to somebody where you can be frank about yourself...talking to somebody does help. As yet, there's no sort of concrete help that she gave me at the time...

Nevertheless, the low ratings given by clients at Service B may give cause for concern, in view of this Service's notion of counselling as a key function and because advisers at both B and C rated counselling much more highly than the clients. At Service A, clients were slightly happier with the counselling than advisers, which may be attributable to the latter's view that they were not really competent to offer this facility. Ratings for Service D show that advisers valued counselling lowest of all the functions, which is surprising in view of the fact that this Service has by far the greatest amount of on-going contact with clients and since it placed substantial emphasis on this function. However, advisers did feel the constraints of time strongly — though it is noted that clients at this Service expressed the strongest satisfaction with this component of the interview.

Overall value

Table 38: Rating of guidance functions: overall value, clients' and advisers' ratings (means)

Service	Client	Adviser
D	8.9	6.7
A	7.0	7.6
B	6.5	7.3
C	8.8	9.1

Table 38 compares the ratings made by clients and advisers of the overall value of the interviews at the four Services. Again it is clear that at three of the four Services, A, B and C, clients expressed less satisfaction with overall value than did the advisers. At Services A, C and D, clients were prepared to rate the overall value as greater than the individual parts, but at Service B, which performed relatively poorly in overall value, information was given a higher value. Service C and D's clients clearly valued highly their contact with their Service overall, though Service C contacts were primarily informational ones. Service C advisers were also most satisfied of all four Services with the overall value of contacts. We believe that this satisfaction is largely attributable to the very concrete nature of information provision. Again, there is a discrepant result at Service D, with advisers rating overall value much lower than clients expressed in using the Service. We believe this reflects the general ease and confidence which clients expressed in using the Service, compared with advisers' vivid awareness of the problems in educational guidance and perhaps an over-sensitivity to their own shortcomings.

Rank orderings

Table 39: Rating of guidance functions: overall rank orderings (means)

Rank order	Interview component	Mean client rating	Interview component	Mean adviser rating
1	Overall value	7.8	Information	8.2
2	Information	7.5	Overall value	7.7
3	Advice	7.2	Advice	7.5
4	Assessment	6.8	Assessment	7.2
5	Counselling	4.4	Counselling	5.4

Table 39 compares the combined ratings of clients and advisers on each of the five aspects of the interview and gives the rank orderings of both parties in terms of levels of satisfaction. The Table shows broad agreement on ranking, except for the inversion of overall value and information.

Table 40: Service A: clients' and advisers' rank orderings of satisfaction (means)

Rank order	Interview element	Mean client rating	Interview element	Mean adviser rating
1	Overall value	7.0	Information	8.0
2	Advice	6.4	Overall value	7.6
3	Information	5.9	Advice	7.1
4	Counselling	5.8	Assessment	7.0
5	Assessment	5.4	Counselling	5.2

Table 41: Service B: clients' and advisers' rank orderings of satisfaction (means)

Rank order	Interview element	Mean client rating	Interview element	Mean adviser rating
1	Information	7.7	Information	7.8
2	Overall value	6.5	Assessment	7.7
3	Advice	6.1	Advice	7.5
4	Assessment	6.0	Overall value	7.3
5	Counselling	4.5	Counselling	6.8

Table 42: Service C: clients' and advisers' rank orderings of satisfaction (means)

Rank order	Interview element	Mean client rating	Interview element	Mean adviser rating
1	Overall value	8.8	Information	9.6
2	Information	8.2	Overall value	9.1
3	Advice	7.8	Advice	8.9
4	Assessment	7.2	Assessment	8.6
5	Counselling	0.3	Counselling	4.7

Table 43: Service D: clients' and advisers' rank orderings of satisfaction (means)

Rank order	Interview element	Mean client rating	Interview element	Mean adviser rating
1	Overall value	8.9	Information	7.2
2	Assessment	8.4	Overall value	6.7
3	Advice	8.3	Advice	6.4
4	Information	8.1	Assessment	5.5
5	Counselling	7.1	Counselling	5.0

Tables 40 to 43 detail the rank orderings for each individual Service. They show that assessment is ranked by clients at Service D much higher than at the other Services, with information somewhat lower. Clients at all four Services are broadly in line in their rankings of advice, overall value and counselling. Advisers' rankings are identical at Services A, C and D, but Service B's rankings invert the assessment and overall value rankings. This reflects perhaps its confidence in this function being achieved as part of the counselling process.

In sum, the picture appears to be one where clients at Services A, B and C find the content of the interviews *less* satisfactory than do the advisers. Clients tend to value overall value and information highest and assessment and counselling lowest. Clients at Service D were *more* satisfied with the interview than advisers, reflecting perhaps the 'befriending' approach of this very client-centred Service and the on-going assistance offered. Advisers at Services A, B and C consistently over-rated the components of the interview for clients, though rank orderings were similar. This over-rating was not at all evident at Service D, reflecting perhaps its greater awareness of the problems inherent in the guidance process outside the immediate interview setting.

CHAPTER THIRTEEN

PROGNOSIS AND OUTCOME

Introduction

We examined advisers' and clients' views of the outcome of interviews in two ways. First, advisers were asked (at the end of their interview with us) to offer a prediction of what clients would do, and how far they might get in pursuit of their aims. Clients were similarly asked to make these predictions. These data are considered in the Prognosis section. Clients were also followed up by individual fieldworkers, after an appropriate period, to ascertain actual as opposed to predicted outcomes. These data are considered in the Outcome section. The final section considers the implications of these findings.

Prognosis

Prognosis made by advisers and clients, at the end of their interviews with us, were compared with actual outcome in an attempt to compare how accurately each party was able to predict what would happen to clients. Table 44 shows that in only one-quarter of all cases did advisers accurately predict the outcome for clients, whether positive or negative. Service A was least successful in this respect, with accurate predictions made in only 15% of its cases, and Service B was most successful, with accurate predictions in 45% of its cases. In the five cases where Service D advisers made predictions, only one accurately reflected outcome; but any inferences which may be drawn are inhibited by the fact that this Service accounts for all the instances of 'No prognosis', whether by clients or advisers, again reflecting its preference for a staged approach to educational guidance. The 'No

Table 44: Prognosis: advisers' and clients' prognosis in accord with outcome

	Adviser		Client	
	Number of cases (n=76)	Total %	Number of cases (n=76)	Total %
Yes	18	24	27	36
No	42	55	35	46
No prognosis	7	9	5	7
No information	9	12	9	12

data' category is accounted for by the nine clients who could not be contacted for follow-up, so that their actual outcome could not be compared with their own, or with their advisers' ratings. Clients were more likely to predict outcome accurately; even so, they were correct in only just over one-third of cases.

The reasons why advisers were inaccurate in their predictions may be related to findings evidenced in earlier chapters, such as incomplete assessments and a tendency to over-rate the value of assistance offered. Clients might underestimate the difficulties ahead; some evidenced a rather fragile motivation towards continuing education, abandoned when an offer of employment was made; and some were subject to chance events in their personal lives which led them in other directions.

Outcome

Following-up of clients was conducted at an appropriate period after the EGSA interview, dependent on the time the fieldwork was conducted and the nature of the enquiry; most were made between four and six months after initial interview. Nine (12%) clients could not be contacted. In most cases, this was because clients were not on the telephone and did not respond to follow-up letters. Information on outcome for three such Service D clients was obtained by reference to the Service's continuing case records.

Table 45 shows the numbers and proportions of clients whose outcomes fell in the broad categories delineated, by individual EGSA and in total. Only sixteen (21%) of the total sample directly used the guidance given and enrolled (and stayed) on a course. A further eleven (14%) took another course which had not been recommended during the EGSA interview. Almost half such clients were from Service C. C4, for example, rejected the full-time options offered her because she could not justify giving up her job when the grant aid available was likely to be very low, and so was taking two 'O' levels part-time. C10 found that her employers had changed their training specification, so she returned to the Service to find an alternative course but wasn't offered one. C10 therefore took up a private course with a local secretarial college, which she found very expensive and poorly taught. This client, at follow-up, was leaving secretarial work to start a two-year training course in nursing, from information gained from her own sources. A few clients in this category changed their minds about what they wanted to do. D2, for example, decided that the course in which he was interested (and entry to which the EGSA had taken pains to negotiate for him) was too long. Rather than train to become a car mechanic, he proposed to pursue the 'Knowledge of London' and become a taxi-driver, which he considered he could accomplish in half the time and which would provide him with work equally viable financially and just as congenial.

147

Table 45: Outcome

Outcome	Service A		Service B		Service C		Service D		All Services	
	Number of clients (n=20)	Total %	Number of clients (n=20)	Total %	Number of clients (n=20)	Total %	Number of clients (n=16)	Total %	Number of clients (n=76)	Total %
1. Took up a course as a result of EGSA interview	4	20	4	20	3	15	5	31	16	21
2. Took up another course	3	15	1	5	5	25	2	13	11	14
3. Took up a recommended course but abandoned it	2	10	2	10	0	0	2	13	6	8
4. Preferred a job offer	2	10	4	20	2	10	0	0	8	11
5. Personal circumstances intervened	1	5	3	15	1	5	1	6	6	8
6. Failed to obtain a suitable course	6	30	2	10	4	20	1	6	13	17
7. Did nothing	2	10	3	15	1	5	0	0	6	8
8. No information	0	0	1	5	4	20	5	31	10	13

148

Six clients proceeded to the recommended course but subsequently abandoned it. The four clients in this category from Services A and B were very dissatisfied with this outcome, as indicated in earlier chapters. But at Service D the two clients expressed no dissatisfaction, either with the course taken or with the Service; they simply preferred to take up offers of employment made to them. A further eight (16%) clients took no direct action on the guidance given, because of finding a job. Most of this group had come to the Service seeking employment rather than continuing education in the first place. Half the group were drawn from Service B, many of whose sample, it will be recalled, had been attracted to the Service by a local radio broadcast which emphasised the vocational implications of further education.

Personal circumstances, such as emigration, moving house or a change in spouse's occupation, intervened in six (8%) cases. Only one of these, B15, had already begun a course.

The thirteen clients who failed to obtain a suitable course at all constituted the second largest category (17%). Nearly half these clients were drawn from Service A, and the next largest group (four) from Service C. Factors contributing to such failure included being unable to obtain grant aid; refusal of admission; lack of places; and lack of suitability in terms of time, course content or conditions of study. All such clients were dissatisfied, wholly or in part, with this outcome. Examples included D4, who was refused a discretionary grant to pursue an art foundation course; A13, whose problems in gaining admission to an 'O' level course are outlined in Chapter 10; and A10, whose recommendations for improving EGSA information are quoted in Chapter 9. C2 failed to take up the option offered because it was an evening class which conflicted with her work shifts. B14 wanted a basic book-keeping course but none was available. C8 failed to take up the language laboratory option offered, as she wanted the support of a group. At the time of follow-up, she had not discovered an alternative, although she had bought a recorded course.

Finally, six (8%) clients did nothing at all. Two of these clients appeared to the fieldworker to be so much at odds with themselves that their result is not surprising; but among the others there was concern that the EGSA contact had not been what they expected and that they had found themselves no further forward.

(One client at Service D was eventually asked not to return since in the adviser's view he was 'extremely persistent...asking us to do the impossible'. His outcome has been included in the 'No information' category).

Implications

In line with American experience, we consider it a most complex task to measure the effectiveness of agencies such as EGSAs, and it would be inappropriate to adopt as sole criterion of success the numbers of clients taking up and staying on courses. That would suggest a too crudely recruitment-oriented role, at odds with EGSAs' views of themselves as essentially client-centred. Moreover, it is clear that a substantial minority of clients in this sample preferred a job to a course; for some, unavoidable personal circumstances intervened; and there were a few for whom one suspects any outcome would have been unsatisfactory. Nevertheless, the substantial majority presented themselves with a primary or a secondary educational intent and in the hope of finding some way forward. While it would be unrealistic to expect that every client should have found an appropriate educational 'answer', it must surely be a matter of concern that so many experienced problems which might have been avoided by more attention to their needs. Such clients were included in the 'Took up another course', 'Took up a recommended course but abandoned it', 'Failed to obtain a suitable course' and 'Did nothing' categories of Table 45. Their experiences point to the necessity for EGSAs to attend more closely first to the assessments they make. Information also needs careful attention, to ensure that it is as complete, accurate and reliable as possible. We note that some clients attempted to resolve their information needs themselves, without further recourse to the EGSA; and that some pursued routes outside the statutory sector. This also has implications for the comprehensiveness of EGSAs' information resources. Advice was sometimes inappropriate or irrelevant; counselling seemed hardly to reach those clients who were in need of it and was sometimes ineffectively provided.

However, it would appear that Service D did succeed in providing a more consistently relevant service and one with which clients were well pleased across all the functions of educational guidance. Its mode of practice differed in many important respects from the other Services studied. Such inferences as may be drawn from this are weakened by the high rate of sample attrition and the smaller case-load; and the particular conditions under which Service D operates may not be applicable to, for example, a rural area. Nevertheless, our researches have pointed up some common weaknesses at Services A, B and C. We consider it is a major deficiency that advisers were so frequently unable to predict accurately their clients' outcomes and/or did not maintain contact with them. A positive approach in this matter not only demonstrates concern for the client (however time-consuming the mechanics of the operation); it may also act as an effective self-monitoring process. Additionally, it provides feedback for providers which may benefit clients, institutions and Services alike.

We consider that the outcomes for many clients in our sample provide ample demonstration that those who have established Services are correct in their belief that adults are greatly in need of the assistance they aim to offer. It is a matter of regret that Services so often have not used the opportunities open to them. In making this

150

point, we are fully aware of the constraints under which these Services operate; yet we consider the issue to be one of policy as much as of funding.

PART 3:CONCLUSIONS AND RECOMMENDATIONS

CHAPTER FOURTEEN

CONCLUSIONS AND RECOMMENDATIONS

The recommendations made in *Links to learning*, reproduced in Appendix 3, appear to us to be very relevant in 1983, except that some encouraging developments since the Report's publication may be noted. First, some Services, particularly those in the London area, are beginning to be 'financed in ways which make coherent planning possible' (iii). We note that EGSAs now are generally 'cooperative and collaborative ventures rather than the exclusive presence of any one professional group or institution' (iv). The National Association of Educational Guidance Services for Adults, founded in 1982, while a voluntary body dependent entirely on subscriptions, has as a central concern the provision of 'a central focus and support for the most effective development of local guidance services' (vi); and it also acts as an information exchange '...to facilitate cooperation and development' (xiii).

The specific focus of our research has been the interaction between adviser and client, rather than issues such as management, structure and funding, although these factors do strongly affect both the operation and the approach to clients. However, in our view there are a number of critical areas of practice which EGSAs must attend to unequivocally from the viewpoint of the interests of the client. It is in the light of this consideration that the conclusions and recommendations which follow are made. They are drawn from the 'Implications' sections in the chapters making up Part 2 of this Report, to which readers interested in the fuller discussion are directed.

1. In view of the heavy demands of time which are required to allow clients to express their needs and advisers fully to comprehend and effectively to enact educational guidance, we consider that over-emphasis on a large through-put of clients is inappropriate. Even enquirers who genuinely have an 'information-only' enquiry need time fully to articulate their needs and advisers need time to assess these needs and to conduct thorough information searches. Many EGSAs told us of the demand for large-scale information events, especially at peak enrolment times. While we accept that these exercises bring valuable publicity and recruitment to EGSAs, they cannot be considered a substitute for a personalised guidance service.

2. EGSAs appear to experience difficulty in attracting multiple-disadvantaged groups as clients. In this respect, the importance of long-term outreach strategies is underlined, which in turn reinforces

155

the great importance of judging EGSAs' impact over a long period of time, since such clients are unlikely to view education as immediately relevant — in the way that those with more successful experience may do. Nevertheless, it is clear that simple strategies, such as publicity at appropriate locations and through the media, may be very effective. In this case, it is essential that the publicity reflects accurately what the EGSA is able to provide, and that personnel referring clients from agencies and institutions have a clear understanding of what the Service does.

3. The overlap between clients' educational and vocational aspirations is often very strong. It means that advisers must have a basic grasp of the training and employment opportunities in the area, but above all, that the strongest possible links are made with the vocational agencies.

4. It is apparent that EGSAs need to consider very carefully how much of the task of educational guidance may be devolved to contacts within providing institutions. It is clearly unrealistic — and unwise — to expect to provide all the assistance a client may need within the confines of the EGSA itself. However, even where such contacts are anticipated to provide only information about their own courses or subject area, they clearly need to be sympathetic to the needs of the aspiring adult student; and we do not consider (except in exceptional cases) that such contacts may be assumed, without extensive training, to be *ipso facto* adequate assessors, advisers or counsellors. Furthermore, in view of the difficulty which these four Services experienced in establishing adequate contact networks, it would appear that devolution is more theoretical than actual, with the main onus of further research placed on clients themselves. In these circumstances, EGSAs may need to reconsider, first, their attention to institutional outreach and second, the role that the Service's centre should play.

5. This raises the question of the type of staff recruited and of staff training. Since there are currently very few experienced and professionally trained educational guidance workers, the importance of developing in-house training and of encouraging staff to attend relevant courses, as in counselling skills, is apparent. We consider that no new Service can be equipped to begin work without a substantial monitored training period; the same applies to new members of staff. It was not possible to conclude from our research that volunteers or MSC or full-time professional staff performed 'best' or 'worst' — only that certain policies and operational conditions ensured a more secure result for the client. We do conclude, however, that untrained staff, even though very experienced in continuing education, do not

inherently and necessarily possess the range and depth of skills essential for educational guidance. Parallels with the early days of the adult literacy movement are apparent.

6. Assessment of clients is conducted largely in a haphazard and sometimes unconscious way, but assessment may have a very substantial impact on outcome. We consider that the systematisation of assessment of clients' personal contexts is essential. These Services have not yet developed such tools, which are especially important where contact with the client is not maintained and where there are large numbers of advisers in a Service's team, with resultant inconsistencies. Staff will need training in the use of such tools, and also in sensitivity towards their own values and biases. We consider in addition that the omission of testing facilities for some clients is inappropriate; in particular, evaluation of clients' general potential is a matter unlikely to be resolved by referring them to course tutors.

7. We consider it very clear from the evidence of this report that a comprehensive information resource is vital to EGSAs' credibility and to clients' outcomes. We have attended in detail to how completeness may be judged at the level of public information, yet that must be considered the basic line from which advisers check the availability of learning opportunities. It is frustrating for clients to be referred to courses which do not exist or have no places available or are simply unsuitable. Advisers need also to be in a position to offer clients information about grant aid and other sources of funding; and to supplement public information with semi-public information which may have a vital bearing on the viability of options selected. We also consider that what clients have to say about their experiences is information which EGSAs can ill afford to ignore. Implicit in these conclusions is an information bank which can reliably be accessed and staff who are skilled in using the bank. They are also likely to benefit from substantial training in the structure and provision of continuing education, including visits to the courses to which referrals are most frequently made.

8. Both advisers and counsellors expressed confusion about the differences between advice and counselling. From the EGSAs' viewpoint, this weakens advisers' ability to identify what the client's needs are; from the clients' viewpoint, it causes difficulty in asserting them. In our view, identifying advice and counselling need is a skill in itself, and not one which may be left to intuition or to a direct request. Again, to be reliable, accurate identification requires training in awareness of the implications of enquiries, underpinned by sound assessment and information competence. Clients are likely to need assistance in seeking advice and in relating the advice given to their aspirations.

Similarly, they may need help in identifying or articulating a counselling need. We have noted that advisers and clients were not in accord about the extent to which counselling was offered during interview, but it is clear that something of this provision was made. In this respect, we feel that the point made in the Russell Report and quoted in Chapter 2 is salutary:

> ...To establish a true counselling service for adult education would be a costly and elaborate undertaking with heavy training demands, for inexpert counselling is potentially harmful.

and *Links to learning* makes the point that '...clients are entitled to be assured of the competence of their counsellors.'[36] The point is clear that if EGSAs are to make a creditable claim to offer counselling to clients, and bearing in mind the responsibility of such a role, then professionalism is an absolute prerequisite. The same considerations apply to all who are asked by the EGSA to provide counselling; not only, that is, to centre staff.

9. Referral is most likely to be appreciated and used by clients where it is direct, named and assisted, which implies that Services must attend carefully to the selection of referral points, not only in quantity but in quality. Where this cannot be assured, then clients are likely to benefit from actions taken directly on their behalf by advisers. We also noted that several clients benefited from (and much appreciated) acts of implementation on their behalf. Services cannot be accurately attuned to the needs of clients for such assistance as advocacy without consistent and thorough attention to follow-up.

10. Follow-up benefits more than the individual client. It provides a salutary insight for the Service itself as to the viability and relevance of its provision; it also provides data for feedback to providers. Failure to attend to this activity detracts from the claims of the Service to be both effective and client-centred, and it weakens its role in amplifying and making coherent the voice of the consumer. That such a role is necessary is amply demonstrated by our research; many clients' outcomes vindicate the importance of a pro-active approach. As a final point, we would add that follow-up is only part of the process of self-monitoring to which the Services in our research gave too little attention. Part of the problem here is that Services are not always clear what should be monitored, why and for whom. Again, American experience may be relevant:

> ...Our mission and services are accountable first and foremost to the needs of learners. Our evaluation efforts must be similarly guided. We seek first to provide evaluation which is most useful to clients...As a second priority, we seek to provide evaluative feedback to staff regarding their impacts...We also seek to provide process evaluation for manage-

158

ment purposes...Finally, we pursue evaluation for the needs of outside agencies, to account for funds received in order to justify and support further funding requests...[37]

In conclusion, we wish to emphasise that any report such as this pays particular attention to development and so may appear critical to those approaching the subject for the first time. The many EGSAs with whom we had contact will be aware that our role has been to support the work they are engaged in — from an understanding of the sometimes appalling circumstances, particularly in the matter of funding, with which they have had to contend. Moreover, at the start of our work, there were only two EGSAs with a lengthy (and very highly respected) operational history behind them. Educational guidance is still a very new concept and one which it is hoped this research will advance, since, at its completion, we are convinced of the vital importance of educational guidance for adults and of the relevance of Services already in operation to a very substantial — and growing — social need.

REFERENCES

1. Irving, A. *Partnerships: libraries, open learning and adult education,* 9–13 July 1979. Loughborough University. (Unpublished).
2. Advisory Council for Adult and Continuing Education. *Links to learning:* a report on educational information, advisory and counselling services for adults. ACACE 1979.
3. Osborn, M., Charnely, A. and Withnall, A. *Educational information, advice, guidance and counselling for adults:* Review of existing research in adult and continuing education Vol VI. National Institute of Adult Education (England and Wales) 1981.
4. Percy, K. A., Langham, M. and Adams, J. G. *Educational information, advisory and counselling services for adults:* a source book. Lancaster Services on Adult Education No 3. University of Lancaster 1982.
5. Ironside, D. J. *Models for counselling adult learners.* Department of Adult Education, Ottawa Institute for Studies in Education 1981.
6. Redmond, M. A. *Why Education Information and Guidance Services for Adults? in* Mercer, R. A. *ed. Educational information and guidance for adults.* Sheffield Papers in Education Management No 16. Department of Education Management, Sheffield City Polytechnic 1981.
7. *Directory of educational guidance services for adults.* 1st edition. ACACE 1981.
8. *Directory of educational guidance services for adults.* 2nd (Revised) edition. ACACE 1982.
9. *Directory of educational guidance services for adults.* 3rd (Revised) edition. ACACE 1983.
10. Michaels, R. *Setting up, developing and sustaining appropriate services for adults. in* Mercer, R. A. *ed. Educational information and guidance for adults,* op. cit.
11. Advisory Council for Adult and Continuing Education, *Continuing education: from policies to practice.* ACACE, 1982.
12. Osborn, M., Charnley, A. and Withnall, A. *Educational information, advice, guidance and counselling for adults,* op. cit.
13. *Adult education: a plan for development.* Report by a Committee of Inquiry appointed by the Secretary of State for Education and Science under the chairmanship of Sir Lionel Russell. HMSO 1973.
14. Percy, K. A., Langham, M. and Adams, J. G. *Educational information, advisory and counselling services for adults,* op. cit.
15. The Open University. *Report of the Committee on Continuing Education.* (Venables Report). Open University, 1976.
16. Advisory Council for Adult and Continuing Education. *Links to learning.* op. cit.
17. Heffernan, J. M., Macy, F. U. and Vickers, D. F. *Educational brokering: a new service for adult learners.* National Centre for Educational Brokering, New York 1976.
18. Advisory Council for Adult and Continuing Education. *Links to learning,* op. cit.
19. Ibid.
20. Ibid.
21. Patterson, A. *Characteristics of Educational Guidance Services. In* Butler, I. et al. *eds. Developing educational information and guidance services for adults.* Sheffield Papers in Education Management No 28. Department of Education Management, Sheffield City Polytechnic, 1983.
22. Department of Education for Northern Ireland. *Educational guidance for adults in Northern Ireland.* (The Jackson Report). HMSO 1979.
23. Michaels, R. *Setting up, developing and sustaining appropriate services for adults. In* Mercer, R. A. *Educational information and guidance for adults,* op. cit.
24. Burton, K. *Tower Hamlets Education Advice:* (Thea). *In* Mercer, R. A. *Educational information and guidance for adults,* op. cit.
25. Ironside, D. J. *Models for counselling adult learners,* op. cit.

26. Advisory Council for Adult and Continuing Education. *Continuing education: from policies to practice,* op. cit.
27. Advisory Council for Adult and Continuing Education. *Links to learning.* op. cit.
28. Butler, L. *Educational guidance for adults: some terms, definitions and issues in the practice of educational guidance by independent services and public libraries.* EASP, 1981.
29. Advisory Council for Adult and Continuing Education. *Links to learning,* op. cit.
30. *Ways and means of strengthening information and counselling services for adult learners:* report of the International Symposium, May 22–27, 1977. University of Southern California College of Continuing Education in conjunction with UNESCO. UNESCO, 1978.
31. Watts, A. G. *Educational and careers guidance services for adults. II: A review of current provision.* British Journal of Guidance and Counselling, Vol. 8 (2), 1980.
32. Ironside, D. J. *Models for counselling adult learners,* op. cit.
33. Gains, D. *The Co-operation of Continuing Education Advisory Services with Libraries. In Adult education and public libraries in the 1980s: A symposium.* Papers given at a special conference organised by the Library Association on 21st February 1979. The Library Association 1980.
34. Heffernan, J. M., Macy, F. U. and Vickers, D. F. *Educational brokering: a new service for adult learners,* op. cit.
35. *Guidelines for a successful brochure.* The Leeds Educational Information for Adults Project. Leeds Polytechnic. 1981.
36. Advisory Council for Adult and Continuing Education. *Links to learning,* op. cit.
37. Heffernan, J. M., Macy, F. U. and Vickers, D. F. *Educational brokering: a new service for adult learners,* op. cit.

APPENDIX 1

INTERVIEW SCHEDULE: PRELIMINARY SURVEY

Introduction

The purpose of the interview is to examine broadly the operational ethos of the service; its structure and functions; and its resources, from the point of view of the practitioner. As a general point, the interview is intended to reflect as much the respondent's views on the functioning of the service as on more theoretical matters. In this respect, it should be emphasised that there are no right or wrong answers.

The areas that we have identified as relevant are intended to form the basis of the interview, but there may well be others which you will want to raise. For this reason, and because so many of the areas overlap and inter-relate with each other, we have produced a check-list of topics on which to base our interview (read check-list through). It may be that, as we talk, you will want to change emphasis or develop points as they arise. We shall also send you a copy of the transcript of the interview, if you wish, in case you want to add further comments on the discussion.

Check-List

1. Background to Service:
   How it came to be set up.
   The needs it was intended to serve.
   The working ethos/general approach of the Service to its task.
2. Structure of Service:
   Type of Structure.
   Relationship with any management body.
   Relationship with other agencies, both educational institutions and other related agencies e.g. Careers.
   Relationship with public library specifically.
3. Resources:
   Funding/resourcing.
   Staffing: type of training.
   Premises used.
   Other specific resources.
4. Functions of Service:
   Information provision:
   Types of information collected, its storage, retrieval, interpretation.
   Assessment: Types of assessment offered and when used.
   Advice: Types of advice offered and when used.
   Counselling: Types of counselling offered and when used.
   Implementation: Types of implementation offered and when used.
5. Use of Service:
   Approach to record-keeping, self monitoring, follow-up.
   Estimated source, numbers and types of clients.
   Publicity and outreach.

APPENDIX 2a
EASP CLIENT SURVEY

QUESTIONNAIRE

Name ....

1. How old were you when you left school? ....

2. What kind of school did you go to? ....

3. Did you have any educational qualifications when you left school?...............................

   (What were they?) ....

   ....

4. Have you gained any other educational or vocational qualifications
   since leaving school?...

   (What are they?)...

   ....

5. How old are you?...

6. Are you married or single?...

7. What is your occupation? ....

   (If not employed what was your previous occupation?)..

   (What is your spouse's occupation?)..

   (If not employed what was your spouse's previous occupation?) ....

   ....

8. Do you have any children?..

   (What are their ages?)...

   (Are those over 16 still in full-time education?) ....

9. Are you a member of the Public Library? ....

163

10. (Apart from those we have already discussed,) have you attempted any educational or vocational courses during the last five years? ....

(What were they?)..

....

11. Have you undertaken any other sustained learning activities over the last five years?

(What were they?)..

....

12. Have you been anywhere else for help or advice with your enquiry this year? ....

(Where have you been?)..

....

APPENDIX 2b
EGSA's RECORD FORM

Name of Client...

Tel No...

Address ....

Visit   ☐

Phone
Call   ☐

Broad nature of enquiry ....

....

Options discussed...

....

Information sources used..

....

Outcomes of enquiry (e.g. supply of address, referral elsewhere)

....

Name of Worker...................................Date ....

APPENDIX 2c
EGSA INTERVIEW SCHEDULE

1. Were you able to make any assessment at all about this client?
   PROMPT: personal (e.g. personality, family); education, employment, abilities/
   potentialities; motivations/aspirations.
   PROMPT: whether assessment was volunteered, requested or intuited.
2. On your form for this client you've listed ....
   for the broad nature of the enquiry and option/s discussed. Could you take me
   through it/them in a little more detail?
3. Did you recommend any options, over and above those discussed, as *most*
   appropriate?
   (Could you just comment on why you felt these to be most suitable?)
4. On your form for this client you've listed ....
   information sources. Could you take me through this in a little more detail?
   PROMPT: use and interpretation of:
                brochures/prospectuses
                directories
                Service's own materials
                use of other professionals/agencies
                worker's personal knowledge
                other.
5. How far do you feel that you were relying on information known to you personally or
   because you are a professional, as opposed to information that was publicly
   available?
   PROMPT: nature of information: public, semi-public, private.
6. Were you involved in counselling with this client at all?
   PROMPT: did you help her/him work towards defining her/his underlying personal
                needs in order to establish what the realistic options were?
7. On your form for this client you've listed ....
   under outcomes. Could you comment on this please?
   PROMPT: actions taken or to be taken by the worker.
                actions taken or to be taken by the client.
8. Approximately how much time did you spend on each of these areas?
   PROMPT: assessment
                : information
                : advice
                : counselling
                : implementation
9. What do you think the client will do now?
   How far do you think s/he will get in her/his intention?
10. Any other comments?

APPENDIX 2d
EGSA's RATINGS SCALE

1. How far do you feel you were able to make an accurate assessment of the client?

....

2. How far do you feel you were able to provide the client with the information s/he needed?

....

3. How far do you feel you were able to give the client the advice s/he needed?

....

4. How far do you feel you were able to give the client the counselling s/he needed?

....

5. As a whole, how valuable do you feel the transaction was for the client?

....

APPENDIX 2e
CLIENT INTERVIEW SCHEDULE

1. Broadly, what were you enquiring about?
   PROMPT: the nature of the enquiry: any particular subjects, modes of study, qualifications.
2. What is it that had made you look for this information at this particular time?
   PROMPT: institutional constraints, e.g. start of courses.
   : short/medium/long-term educational aspirations.
   : short/medium/long-term vocational aspirations.
   : changes in personal circumstances, e.g. redundancy.
   : unfinished business.
3. What made you come to the EGSA for help with your enquiry?
   PROMPT: occasion of use; expectations.
4. Did the adviser make any assessment of you?
   PROMPT: personal (e.g. personality, family); education, employment, abilities/ potentialities; motivations/aspirations.
   PROMPT: whether assessment was volunteered, requested or intuited.
5. Could you take me through the options you discussed (if any) in a little more detail?
6. Were any recommended as the most suitable for you?
   Have you any comments on why this was so?
7. What information was provided for you on each option?
   PROMPT: use and interpretation of:
   brochures/prospectuses
   directories
   service's own materials
   use of other professionals/agencies
   worker's personal knowledge
   other.
8. Was the adviser able to give you information other than what was available from the brochures and so on?
   PROMPT: nature of information: public, semi-public, private.
9. If you were given printed information to take away, how helpful has it been to you?
   PROMPT: content, layout, comprehensibility.
10. did your contact with the adviser include any counselling?
    PROMPT: did the adviser help you work towards defining your underlying personal needs in order to establish what the realistic options were?
11. What was the outcome of your enquiry?
    PROMPT: supply of information/referral
    : further actions by worker/client.
12. What do you think you will do now?
    How far do you think you will get in your intention?
13. It is sometimes difficult for people like yourself to find the kind of educational information and advice they need. How do you think things might be improved?
    PROMPT: improvements in Service used
    : other improvements

APPENDIX 2f
CLIENTS' RATINGS SCALE

1. How far do you feel the adviser was able to make an accurate assessment of you?

....

2. How far do you feel the adviser was able to provide you with the information you needed?

....

3. How far do you feel the adviser was able to give you the advice you needed?

....

4. How far do you feel the adviser was able to give you the counselling you needed?

....

5. As a whole, how valuable do you feel the transaction was for you?

....

APPENDIX 3
RECOMMENDATIONS FROM 'LINKS TO LEARNING'

The Advisory Council appreciates that recommendations for the development of new services in times of economy will be even more stringently examined and costed than in times of prosperity. The foregoing report and the following recommendations have been written in that knowledge. We have already made clear, and repeat in the first recommendation below, that educational guidance services for adults are essential to the development of continuing education. The other recommendations appear to us inescapable if these guidance services are to become widespread and effective.
Paragraph numbers refer to the directly relevant paragraphs in the preceding text (of Links to learning).

General
(i) Educational guidance services for adults should be recognised as the crucial link between the educational needs and demands of adults and the learning opportunities offered by education providers (paragraph 14).
(ii) Local guidance services should pay particular attention to those clients' educational demands which may not always be capable of being met by existing educational provision (paragraphs 14, 15 and 46).
(iii) Local guidance services should be financed in ways which make coherent planning possible. Current initiatives in providing local guidance services should be given guaranteed support over three or four years to allow their development to be independently monitored (paragraphs 51 and 58).
(iv) Local guidance services should be co-operative and collaborative ventures rather than the exclusive preserve of any one professional group or institution (paragraph 57).

Central Government
(v) The Department of Education and Science and the Welsh Office should make clear the importance which they attach to the development of these local guidance services for adults (paragraph 17).
(vi) A national agency should be sponsored to provide a central focus and support for the most effective development of local guidance services (paragraphs 58 to 62 and Appendix 8).
(vii) The basic financial responsibility for local guidance services should be with local education authorities, and consideration should be given to the inclusion of these costs in the calculations of the Rate Support Grant (paragraph 62).

Local Authorities
(viii) The annual education budgets should make financial and staffing provision for local guidance services, and both initial and in-service teacher training budgets should provide for the training of staff in the skills needed in these services (paragraphs 43 and 62).
(ix) Urgent attention should be given to the precarious financial state of many existing educational guidance services (paragraph 51).

Institutional Providers of Education for Adults
(x) All institutions providing educational opportunities for adults should offer active support to the establishment and development of local guidance services (paragraph 57).

(xi) The content, style and dissemination of information and publicity material about educational opportunities for adults should be continually reviewed, with more effective use being made of broadcasting and of informal social networks (paragraphs 22 to 28 and Appendix 3).

(xii) More opportunities should be provided for adults to relate their own abilities and aspirations to the education provision open to them and so make their own choices within it (paragraph 33).

Organisers of Local Educational Guidance Services for Adults

(xiii) More effective ways should be found to exchange information and experience amongst existing local guidance services so as to facilitate co-operation and development (paragraph 55).

(xiv) Organisations collaborating in local guidance services should be involved in their management, but care should be taken to ensure that the services remain sensitive to the needs and demands of their clients (paragraphs 45 and 46).

(xv) Local guidance services' objects and functions should be clearly defined and records maintained to permit informed judgements on the extent to which they are fulfilling their responsibilities to their clients and to their collaborating institutions (paragraphs 50 and 52 to 54).

(xvi) Local guidance services should be located in places which are easily accessible and inviting to enter (paragraph 41).

(xvii) Some staff with professional guidance skills should be involved in the running of local guidance services so as to establish and maintain acceptable standards of provision and arrange the training of other staff (paragraphs 42 to 44).

(xviii) Local guidance services should make full use of the expertise and goodwill of the LEA Careers Service and other careers guidance services (paragraphs 37 and 38).

(xix) Local guidance services should pay attention to the advantages and disadvantages of the use of computerised data banks (paragraphs 29 to 31 and Appendix 4).

Broadcasters

(xx) Consideration should be given to ways of increasing the effectiveness of broadcasting in providing educational information, in stimulating public awareness, and in encouraging collaboration with and amongst local guidance services (paragraph 28).

Staff Training Institutions

(xxi) Training courses for teachers and administrators in post-school education should provide for the understanding and skills required in undertaking educational guidance work (paragraph 43).

(xxii) In the training of careers officers more attention should be paid to the understanding and skills required in the educational guidance of adults (paragraph 36).

ADVISORY COUNCIL MEMBERSHIP